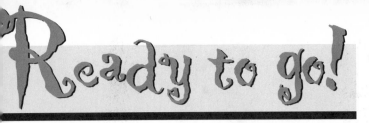Ready to go!

WORD GAMES FOR LITERACY

KS2

P4 to 7

Mrs Tait 3T.

AUTHOR
Martin Coles

EDITORS
Steven Carruthers and
Jean Coppendale

ASSISTANT EDITORS
Dulcie Booth and
Roanne Davis

SERIES DESIGNER
Anna Oliwa

DESIGNER
Anna Oliwa

ILLUSTRATIONS
Phil Dobson

COVER ARTWORK
Andy Parker

**Text © 2001 Martin
Coles**
© 2001 Scholastic Ltd

Designed using Adobe Pagemaker
Published by Scholastic Ltd, Villiers House, Clarendon
Avenue, Leamington Spa, Warwickshire CV32 5PR

234567890   234567890

British Library Cataloguing-in-Publication Data
A catalogue record for this book is available from the
British Library.

ISBN 0-439-01778-5

Contents

Introduction

PLAYING GAMES

We all play games. Everyone plays with language or responds to language play – jokes and puns in conversation, television and radio game shows, crossword puzzles, playground rhymes, advertisements, nonsense poems and word play in newspaper headlines are all examples of the universality of word games. The board game *Scrabble* is now one of the most widely played games in the western world. It has a world championship and associated books of commentary just like chess! Playing with words involves all sorts of positive notions: enjoyment, entertainment, intellectual satisfaction and social rapport. It seems that the impulse to play with words is a very strong one and this book contains practical ideas for simple language games that are intended to capitalize upon that impulse.

Childhood, particularly, is a time of play with language as with much else. Children's rhymes and riddles and word play games are preserved sometimes across centuries. Joke fashions arise spontaneously amongst children, gain currency, and then fade. Evidence of children playing with language, with rhythms and sounds and conventions and taboos, can be gathered from any playground. It is difficult to escape the conclusion that language play is an important element in language development. Piaget and Vygotsky, amongst others, have drawn the attention of educationalists to the idea that play is practice: children enjoy playing with the skills that they are in the process of acquiring. Another famous child psychologist, Jerome Bruner, has said that language is 'most daring and most advanced when it is used in a playful setting' ('Language, Mind and Reading').

CREATIVE USE OF LANGUAGE

The games in this book are intended to engage children and set them free to enjoy learning about language based on play and humour. For good reasons we now no longer attempt to increase competence in language through the kind of instruction represented by repetitive exercises of the sort that existed in old-fashioned grammar books.

However, opportunities for creative use of language are still too few. HMI reports have observed how, once children are competent writers and readers, the range and variety of their written work is undemanding and often still focused on unprofitable comprehension exercises. Yet, in order to learn new language children need a great variety of stimuli and they need to meet language in a range of different contexts. The games and activities in this book provide one set of such contexts. They help children to generate language, they make creative linguistic demands on participants and they increase the range and variety of language work in the classroom. Most importantly, they give children the chance to experiment with language.

The idea that word play is a fundamental part of children's development as language users has long been acknowledged by official reports and curricula. For instance a government report on the teaching of English in 1984 explicitly encourages the use of word games: 'People in general are curious about the workings of language, and English lessons should build on that curiosity. Children in particular are fascinated by word games – by puns, backslang, tongue-twisters, conundrums, double meanings, anagrams, palindromes, etymologies and 'secret' languages.' (The Kingman Report)

More recently the requirements of the national curriculum in England and Wales suggest that: 'Pupils' vocabulary should be extended through activities that encourage their interest in words, including exploration…of word games.' (The National Curriculum: Programme of Study for English) Similarly the range of work for each term in the National Literacy Strategy in England and Wales contains a number of pointers towards using word games during the Literacy Hour. For instance, the programme for Year 6 Term 3 reads: 'to experiment with language, creating new words, similes and metaphors' and Year 3 Term 3 mentions: 'play with language, word puzzles, puns, riddles'. This book contains activities that clearly match these requirements.

CONFIDENCE IN USE OF LANGUAGE

Word games have a liberating force and therefore have a major part to play in developing confidence in language. They allow children to feel that they have power over words, that they can devise and revise, and that it pays to take risks with language. A player has the security of the boundaries imposed by the rules of the game, but on the other hand the freedom to think creatively within these rule boundaries. In word games of the sort offered in this book the child is freed from the burden of having to pay attention to spelling, grammar, punctuation, handwriting and content all at once and can gain confidence by concentrating upon one aspect of language only. Without the worry that inexperience will be mistaken for stupidity and without the threat of correction much can go on which is experimental and open to revision and expansion.

USING THE GAMES IN THE CLASSROOM

Of course, there are dangers in the use of games in the classroom. If used injudiciously they can themselves become a routine that offer too little sense of order and structure to a child's learning. But of course these games will not be the sole content of a child's language curriculum. They offer an additional teaching dimension, one that might be integrated into the Literacy Hour if you teach in England or Wales, but for occasional rather than daily use.

Many of the games will work best with small groups of children. If children work collaboratively they can, to some extent, resolve the problem that all writers have, of being cut off from the stimulus and review of listeners. But group work is not essential, and many games can be played individually, in pairs, or as a whole class.

All of the activities contained here have been tried out with classes either by the author, or by other teachers. Nevertheless, in some circumstances they will require adaptation. This is a book of practical ideas, but those ideas should not be implemented blindly. It would be foolish to suggest that all the ideas will work equally well with all children. Teachers need to use their characteristic energy and creativity to select from the book what they feel able to use and then adapt it or develop the idea. They should feel free to take any game and change it, reorganize it, combine it, distort it or modify it so that it meets the needs of the children in their class. By doing this they should be able to offer individuals an element of enjoyable challenge which is variable in the degree of that challenge, as opposed to offering standard activities regardless of individual differences.

WORD GAMES ACROSS THE CURRICULUM

Some of the games will have a use in curriculum areas other than English. For instance, those games that focus on vocabulary development may be used to help build a corpus of technical words associated with a history or geography topic. Other games require successful collaboration and would be appropriate for PSHE sessions. The skills index on page 64 can be consulted to find games suitable for a variety of purposes and curricular areas. Similarly, although the most of the games require the use of paper and pencils, pupils with access to a computer might choose a word-processing program as a recording tool or, for example, to check their spelling. With a little inventiveness, many ways can be found of giving practice in ICT skills while playing the games. For example, children in schools with intranets could exchange answers via e-mail.

You will know that children are enjoying playing with language and developing their own interests in it when they invent their own variants of the games, and new approaches to the activities. Indeed it is to be hoped that once a range of these games have been introduced to the children and have become part of classroom life, children will realize that classroom language activity does not have to be teacher-initiated and teacher-directed. It is hoped too that they will be encouraged to engage in their own games, invented or modified from the ones they have been taught.

A steady diet of word games is unlikely to ensure the literacy development of any child. What the occasional word game can do is encourage a lively interest in language and the tools of the trade of using it. It can help to develop children's ability to use words more confidently in order to communicate, celebrate, investigate and do a myriad of things that language allows us to do in the classroom and outside it.

Teachers normally try to offer children learning activities that they will enjoy, but this is not the same thing as having fun. With language, the distinction between enjoyment and fun is chiefly a matter of willingness or otherwise to engage in word play. All teachers know the child who sits hunched over his book, tongue over bottom lip, brow furrowed. Above all the games in this book are an attempt to say to that child especially: *Sit up. Smile. Language is fun!*

REFERENCES

Bruner, J 'Language, Mind and Reading' in Goelman, H; Oberg, A; Smith, F (eds): *Awakening to Literacy*, Heinemann, 1984
Report of the Committee of Inquiry into the Teaching of English (*The Kingman Report*), HMSO, 1988
The National Literacy Strategy: Framework for Teaching, DfEE/QCA, 1998
The National Curriculum (Key Stages 1–4), DfEE/QCA, 1999

Section 1 — GAMES WITH LETTERS

It is now widely accepted that children need to be able to discriminate letter sounds as one component in the range of strategies they will use to read. The games in this section will allow you to provide variety in the teaching of sounds in spoken words and knowledge of the alphabetic code. They give you an opportunity to draw to children's attention common spellings for phonemes, correct letter formation and the way in which words can be segmented for spelling.

The activities in this section focus particularly upon:
■ consolidating understanding of alphabetic order
■ providing opportunities to practise finding their way around a dictionary
■ practising visual discrimination and segmentation of words
■ encouraging children to recognise the sounds of letters in speech, listening carefully to and discriminating individual letter sounds
■ encouraging children to look carefully at words, find letter strings, and build an awareness of letter patterns within words, thereby helping them to improve their spelling by leading them towards an understanding of the probability of certain letters occurring in sequence.

ALPHABET GAME

OBJECTIVES

To enable children to:
■ consolidate their understanding of alphabetical order
■ encourage co-operation
■ reinforce their knowledge and spelling of proper nouns.

RESOURCES AND CLASSROOM ORGANIZATION

This activity may require a brief introduction to remind children about the alphabet, the names of the letters and their correct order. As space is required, it might be best carried out around the edge of the classroom or in the hall. You will need to supervise this activity to ensure that the different groups understand the instructions they are given.

This activity is suitable for groups within the whole class.

WHAT TO DO

The children should be organized into groups of five or six. Each group forms a single line according to an instruction from you relating to alphabetical order. For example:
■ Line up in order of the first letter of your first name.
■ Line up in order of the first letter of your last name.
■ Line up in order of the first letter of your street name.
■ Line up in order of the first letter of the month of your birthday.

You could introduce an element of competition into this activity by seeing which group is first to complete their line up correctly.

DIFFERENTIATION

Less able children could be given cards with the appropriate letter of the alphabet to help them. More able groups might be asked to play the game without speaking, or two able groups might be joined together into a larger group to make the task more difficult. In cases where the first letter of the children's names is the same (such as Jenny, John and Josh), some children will be able to sort using the second or even the third letter. Individuals who are confident with alphabetical order might be appointed as referees to check groups have arranged their lines accurately.

NOW OR LATER

Ask the children to write down their own instruction for an alphabetic order to give to another group, and play the game using the children's instructions.

THE THREE SYLLABLE GAME

RESOURCES AND CLASSROOM ORGANIZATION

You may need to introduce this activity by reminding the children what syllables are and how words can be divided in units or syllables. You could write some examples on a board or flip chart. You will need to prepare a list of ten to fifteen three-syllable words in advance.

Supervision will be required as this game can be noisy. It can be played by the whole class or in large groups.

OBJECTIVES

To enable children to:
■ consolidate their understanding that letter groups form syllables that make up a word
■ practise spelling skills.

WHAT TO DO

Choose one, or a few children, to be guessers and tell them to go out of earshot for a short time. Give the rest of the children a three-syllable word, for example, *elephant*, *injection* or *gentleman*. Now divide the children into three groups, giving each a different syllable. The guessers now return, and the three groups all say their syllable once, all at the same time. The guessers must see if they can put the word together. If they fail, the three groups repeat their syllable and the guessers try again. The activity is repeated until the word is solved.

DIFFERENTIATION

For younger or less able children, play the game using two-syllable words, or use three-syllable words but ask the three groups to say each syllable in reverse order rather than at the same time.

NOW OR LATER

Those who are confident with syllables could choose their own three-syllable words for the three groups to say. They could draw up a list of these by skim-reading and picking suitable words from fiction or non-fiction texts.

INVENTED ACRONYMS

RESOURCES AND CLASSROOM ORGANIZATION

This activity will require a brief introduction to explain the concept of acronyms. You could write some examples on a board or flip chart to amplify your explanation. Prepare some examples of acronyms in advance. You will need a copy of photocopiable page 18 for each child or pair, dictionaries, writing materials and paper.

The children can work in pairs or small groups.

OBJECTIVE

To enable children to: recognize and understand acronyms.

WHAT TO DO

Introduce the word 'acronym', explaining that sometimes we make words out of the first letters of other words to avoid repetition and also to help us remember them. For example: SATs (standard assessment tests), SCUBA (self-contained underwater breathing apparatus) and CD-ROM (compact disc – read-only memory).

Discuss some other examples of acronyms with the class. Then divide the children into pairs or small groups and distribute copies of photocopiable page 18. For the first part of this activity, the children will need to use a dictionary to find out what the different acronyms mean. Many dictionaries have an appendix of abbreviations that includes acronyms.

In the second part of the activity, the children have to make up their own acronyms. For example: instead of *working in groups* the children might have *WIGS*. You might ask children to put their work on a *FAP* (*finished assignment pile*), and a class reading session might be the time for *ERIC* (*everyone reading in class*). *SPOT* could be the *Society for the Protection of Toys* (or teachers!), while *CATCH* could be *Can all the class help?*

Answers to photocopiable page 18
UN: United Nations
RAF: Royal Air Force
NATO: North Atlantic Treaty Organization
LASER: Light amplification by stimulated emission of radiation
CAD: Computer-aided design
ERNIE: Electronic random number indicator equipment
BA: Bachelor of Arts
SIS: Secret Intelligence Service
AWOL: Absent without official leave
WHO: World Health Organization
WYSIWYG: What you see is what you get

DIFFERENTIATION

Less able children could work in two groups and make lists of acronyms using dictionaries before they complete photocopiable page 18. These lists could be used to support that activity or used in a quiz with one group playing against the other.

More able children could be asked to use reference books to discover more complicated acronyms.

NOW OR LATER

Start your own class collection of acronyms. These could be kept in a class book or put up on a wall display, or made into a puzzle such as a crossword.

TRAVELLERS' TALES

OBJECTIVES

To enable children to:
■ listen to letter sounds
■ consolidate their knowledge of the alphabet
■ improve their skills with dictionaries and atlases.

RESOURCES AND CLASSROOM ORGANIZATION

You will need to introduce this activity to remind the children about the different parts of speech: proper nouns, nouns, adjectives and verbs. You will need a board or flip chart on which to prepare model answers to show the children as you explain what they have to do in this game. You will also need writing materials, paper, atlases and dictionaries.

Children work in groups for this activity.

WHAT TO DO

Write the following questions and model answer for the letter e on the board for the class to see:

> Where are you going?
> I'm going to England (*proper noun*).
> What will you do there?
> Eat (*verb*) some edible (*adjective*) eels (*noun*).

Now give each child a letter of the alphabet. You could begin by assigning one child the first letter of his or her name. For example: Natalie would be given *n* and the next child *o* and so on. When you reach the end of the alphabet, start over again with *a* until everyone has a letter (you may wish to omit letters *q*, *x* and *z*). Divide the children into groups of five or six. Now, using the model you have provided, ask the children to write examples of their own using their assigned letter and the parts of speech. They can consult dictionaries and atlases to help them. When everyone has finished, the whole group asks each child in turn (starting with Natalie, perhaps!), *Where are you going?* Natalie might answer, *Nigeria* or *Nepal*, or any other country starting with the letter *n*. The group then asks, *What will you do there?* Natalie might answer, *Nibble some nice nuts.*

DIFFERENTIATION

More able children can discuss the construction of the model for the letter e – using the terms 'nouns', 'proper nouns', 'adjectives' and 'verbs'. These children could work in pairs or small groups and try to identify the different parts of speech in each other's answers. Ask the pairs to swap their answers on paper, and then each must write *noun*, *proper noun*, *adjective* and *verb* under the appropriate word in their partner's answer.

Less able children could work in pairs and be given their letter on a piece of paper, together with a list of suggestions of nouns and verbs beginning with their letter. They could use these suggestions to make up their answers.

NOW OR LATER

Play the game again but make inventing an answer more challenging by using capital cities rather than countries, or insist that the noun in the answer is the name of an animal. For example:

> Where are you going?
> I'm going to Paris.
> What will you do there?
> Paint some pink panthers.

FINGER ALPHABET MESSAGES

RESOURCES AND CLASSROOM ORGANIZATION

You will need to learn the American version of the signed alphabet for this lesson. An introduction is required to the whole class to help the children understand the concept of communicating through hand signals and signing. You will need an enlarged copy of the American manual alphabet on photocopiable page 19 for display, a copy for each pair or group, writing materials and paper.

The children should work in pairs or groups of three to five.

WHAT TO DO

Display the enlarged copy of photocopiable page 19. Discuss with the children the variety of ways in which people communicate, including the use of hand signals by referees in sport, traffic police, people waving to each other and so on. Demonstrate some of these signals and ask the children what messages the different signals are conveying.

Explain that some people who are unable to hear sounds communicate using the manual alphabet. Demonstrate by signing a simple two- or three-letter word, saying each letter as you sign it. Then sign one or two simple words and ask the class to identify each letter from the chart on display and then say the word.

Give out the copies of photocopiable page 19 to the pairs or groups. One child should write a very simple message on paper, and then communicate it by signing each letter to their partner (who should keep a written record).

DIFFERENTIATION

Competent spellers could be asked to spell out and decode messages, referring to the manual alphabet sheet, but without writing the letters down.

NOW OR LATER

Children who are successful at using signing can demonstrate to the whole class, perhaps by learning a class member's name in sign language and then asking class to work out whose name it is they are signing.

OBJECTIVES

To enable children to:
■ understand the need for accuracy of spelling
■ practise spelling of known words
■ consolidate their knowledge of the alphabet
■ learn the signing alphabet.

ANAGRAMS, ADDAGRAMS, ROLLAGRAMS AND BACKWORDS

OBJECTIVES

To enable children to:
- recognize and understand anagrams
- consolidate spelling skills
- learn new vocabulary
- practise using a dictionary.

RESOURCES AND CLASSROOM ORGANIZATION

This activity requires an introduction to ensure that the children understand what anagrams are and how they can be solved. Prepare a variety of anagrams for the children to solve. You will need a board or flip chart, paper, writing materials and dictionaries.

This activity is suitable for groups or the whole class.

WHAT TO DO

Introduce this activity by explaining to the whole class that an anagram is a word, or a phrase, formed by changing the order of the letters to form a different word. For example you could write on the board: *meat* is an anagram of *team*, *easel* is an anagram of *lease* and *shore* is an anagram of *horse*. There are a number of games that can be played to give children practice in devising anagrams.

Divide the class into two groups and ask one half to devise anagrams for the other half to solve. Allow them to use a dictionary for reference. If the words and phrases become longer and the anagrams become more ambitious, the children may need clues to help them to solve the anagrams. For example:

Anagram: *hire tent*	**Anagram:** *sirs match*
Clue: *a number*	**Clue:** *a seasonal festival*
Answer: *thirteen*	**Answer:** *Christmas*

DIFFERENTIATION

Less able children could work in pairs for support and be given simple anagrams to solve with picture clues instead of word clues to help them.

'Backwords' is a simple game to extend more able children. It requires them to use a dictionary, or to skim-read text of any kind, to find words that can be read backwards as well as forwards. The discovered word does not have to be a palindrome (the same backward as forwards); *pot* is as acceptable as *pop*. A collection of these words might look something like this: *star, trap, dog, peep, snap, won, on.*

'Addagrams' is a game that is really an extension of 'Anagrams', again for more able children. Divide the children into small groups. Ask one child to write a two- or three-letter word and then the others use those three letters plus one more to make a different word. Another letter is then added to the four letters to make a five-letter word and so on until the group gets stuck. For example:

Starter word: *mat*	**Starter word:** *at*
Turn 1 is *mat + e = team*	**Turn 1** is *it + h = hat*
Turn 2 is *team + s = steam*	**Turn 2** is *hat + s = hats*
Turn 3 is *steam + r = stream*	**Turn 3** is *hats + e = heats*
Turn 4 is *stream + m = stammer*	**Turn 4** is *heats + m = Thames*

'Switch-a-letter' is a similarly challenging anagram game where the object is to transform a given word, by simply switching one letter at a time, to make a different word. Each step must form an actual word. For example: starter word is *have*, which turn by turn can become *hare, hard, lard, land, lane, line, pine, pane*, and so on.

NOW OR LATER

'Rollagram' is a game that can be played by groups of children of all abilities and without supervision. The children will need a set of dice with letters instead of numbers. You can make these by writing six different letters of the alphabet on small squares or circles of sticky paper and placing them over the numbers on an ordinary dice. The number of dice used in the game can vary, but six is perhaps the best. Two of the dice should contain the vowels plus the letter s.

Players take turns to roll all the dice at the same time and the rest of the group write down the letters and try individually to make a word from the letters rolled. Each letter used in a word scores one point so the more words that can be made, and the longer the words discovered, the more points are scored. Use an egg-timer when the dice are rolled to determine the length of time that players have to compose their words.

SINGING LETTERS

RESOURCES AND CLASSROOM ORGANIZATION
You will need to source a variety of simple, well-known songs that have repeated words or phrases.

This activity is teacher-led. The children work as a whole class or in large groups.

WHAT TO DO
During a singing session ask the children to carry out some simple actions whenever they hear a word starting with a particular sound. For example: sing 'My Bonnie Lies Over the Ocean', and whenever the children hear a *b* sound they must stand up. When they next hear a *b* they should sit down. Continue this way (with much laughter) until the song is over.

Choose other letters in other songs and other actions such as *Hands on heads* or *Fold your arms*. As an addition when singing nursery rhymes or other familiar songs, you could change the first consonant of some words and ask the class to identify the letter you have used. For example, you might sing, *Trondon Tridge is talling town*, or *Bumpty, Bumpty, bat on a ball*.

DIFFERENTIATION
Confident children can be asked to invent their own versions of nursery rhymes with changed consonants and then perform them to the class.

NOW OR LATER
'Clap stamp' is a game for children of all abilities. Ask the class to listen for a letter such as *k*. Tell them to clap if the *k* sound is at the beginning of the word and to stamp if it is at the end. Then name a list of words that contain that letter, such as *kite*, *back*, *trick*, *kangaroo* and *kick*. This game can be extended to include double letter sounds and more difficult words.

OBJECTIVE
To enable children to:
recognize the sounds of
letters in words and speech.

GHOST

RESOURCES AND CLASSROOM ORGANIZATION
This activity requires an introduction and explanation. Each group will need a dictionary for reference.

This game should be played in small groups of five or six, sitting in a circle.

WHAT TO DO
'Ghost' is a game that will be familiar to many children. It is easy to play but more difficult to explain.

Step by step, it is played in this way: the first player in the circle says a letter that starts any word they can think of. The second player says the second letter, having

OBJECTIVES
To enable children to
■ practise spelling
■ learn likely and unlikely
letter combinations.

thought of a word that begins with these two letters (at this stage in the game there could be hundreds) but does not say aloud the word they have in mind. The third player then adds another letter, making a combination of three letters that might form the start of a word they have thought of. The fourth player must think of a letter to add to the other three to make a longer word. However, the fourth letter must not complete the word and the fourth player must not say their word unless challenged by the next player in the circle. So, if Player 5 cannot think of a five-letter word or thinks Player 4 is bluffing then they can challenge Player 4 to state the word.

The game continues, around the circle, until someone 'has one ghost' by unintentionally finishing a word, or by being unable to think of a letter to add to the word being spelled.

When a player has three ghosts they are out of the game. For example:

Player 1: *l* **Player 2:** *e* **Player 3:** *a* **Player 4:** *r*	**Player 5:** *The only letter I can think of is 'n' which completes the word. I'm sure that player 4 must have had the word 'learn' in mind, so I couldn't challenge. I have one ghost.*	**Player 4:** *Yes, but I realize now that I should have challenged player 3 because 'lea' is a finished word. So I should have a ghost as well.*

DIFFERENTIATION

This game can be made easier for less able children by allowing two- and three-letter words to stand, and only giving out ghosts for the completion of four- of five-letter words. Appoint children who are confident at using a dictionary to act as referees for the games. They could also keep score and check when there is a dispute about the spelling of a particular word.

As a variation, the game can be played in reverse. One player gives the first letter of a word they have in mind, without mentioning the word. The second player, who may be thinking of a different word, gives the second letter, and so on. The first player to complete a word of more than three letters is the winner. As before, challenges are allowed to ensure all players have permissible words in their heads when adding letters.

NOW OR LATER

Organize a 'Ghost' tournament, with representatives of teams playing each other in groups. The team with the fewest number of ghosts after an agreed number of games wins.

ALPHABETICAL SUITCASE

OBJECTIVES

To enable children to:
■ consolidate their knowledge of the alphabet, as an exercise in concentration
■ confirm knowledge of initial and final letters of words.

RESOURCES AND CLASSROOM ORGANIZATION

Having explained to the children what they have to do, you will need to supervise the game as it is being played.

The game should be played by the whole class, or in a large group, sitting in a circle.

WHAT TO DO

'Suitcase' is one of those well-known games that can be played at all levels of development. In 'Alphabetical suitcase', the simplest version, each player in turn around the circle says *In my suitcase I packed a…* The first player 'puts in' an item starting with the letter *a*, the second player 'puts in' something with a *b*, the third with *c* and so on. In this game, as with all alphabetical games, it should be permitted to substitute *ex* when the letter *x* is reached.

Children who can manage this version of the game easily can be asked to pack their suitcase with a certain category of objects only. For example, they must only pack items:

- found in the home
- needed for a holiday abroad
- that start with the same letter as their first name.

A certain amount of leniency is necessary to give the game speed.

DIFFERENTIATION

More able children could try playing the game in alphabetical reverse starting with the letter *z*.

Older children will be able to play another version of 'Alphabetical suitcase' where they have to repeat everything that is already in the suitcase in the correct order, before adding their own item. If a player forgets an item they are out of the game and the next player has a turn.

Older children will also be able to play 'Bumper-to-bumper suitcase'. As the title suggests, each player has to start their word with the last letter of the item in the suitcase given by the previous player. For example:

> **Player 1:** *In my suitcase I packed a cap.*   **Player 3:** *In my suitcase I packed a loaf.*
> **Player 2:** *In my suitcase I packed a pencil.*   **Player 4:** *In my suitcase I packed a flower.*

and so on.

NOW OR LATER

Children who can play 'Bumper-to-bumper suitcase' will certainly be able to make word chains.

- Variation one: the children could write word chains with the last letter of one word acting as the first letter of the next. They will find it easier and more interesting if the word chain is drawn as a set of steps. An element of competition can be added if groups or pairs of children compete against each other to produce the longest staircase (without using a dictionary). For example: *Bag–grow–window–wet–today–yesterday* and so on.

Bag
   grow
      window
         wet
           today
             yesterday

- Variation two: Ask the children to try and make a word chain using the final two letters of each word. For example: *Chair–irate–team–America–candle.*

Then try using three letters and so on. Using this technique you can make word chains that, if

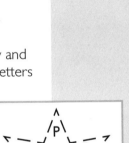

written on joined strips of paper, reach all the way round the classroom. Very able children will be able to design intricate tracks that weave in and out of each other.

- Variation three: children who have designed simple word patterns can be introduced to other possibilities for word patterns. For example: stars and crosses:

SECRET MESSAGES

RESOURCES AND CLASSROOM ORGANIZATION

You will need to make a brief introduction for this activity and show the children some examples of secret messages on a board or flip chart before they play. You will need to have an alphabet line on display in the classroom, writing materials and paper.

The children work initially as individuals, then in pairs.

OBJECTIVE

To enable children to: practise applying alphabetic knowledge and problem-solving skills.

13

WHAT TO DO

Model a secret message to the class. For example:
Explain the various techniques that were used to make these clues: give a word and add to or delete one letter, put two syllables together, 'rhymes with', the place of the letter in the alphabet. Of course, other techniques are possible and the children may want to invent their own.

Using the alphabet line, ask the children to invent their own individual messages. These can also be displayed for others to decipher. Over the course of the day or a week, the messages could be swapped so that a partner could find the solution.

> Add **p** to the front of **lease**.
> Take **b** off **bit** and put **s** in its place.
> Think of the letter before **b**, the letter after **m**, and the letter between **c** and **e**.
> Add **en** to the end of **list**.
> Take the **w** from **two**.
> A word that rhymes with **tea**.

DIFFERENTIATION

You could extend this activity by presenting examples of the different ways in which codes can be designed. Then ask the children to send messages in code to each other. There are many variations to use for letter codes:

> You can make one by leaving gaps in the wrong place:
> *Ple asesi tandli stent ome.*
> By writing words backwards:
> *Esaelp tis dna netsil ot em.*
> By inserting one or two less common letters at intervals:
> *Plexase sqit qand lixstqen toq mex.*
> By swapping each letter with its neighbour, the first with the second, third with fourth, fifth with sixth and so on:
> *Lpaees isa tdn iltsne ot em.*

It is also possible to invent a code using a book. The encoder writes three numbers to identify one word: the page number, the line number and the word number on that line. So the coded message is a list of three connected numbers. Of course, the decoder must use the same book to turn the numbers back into words.

Children will also enjoy 'Reveal-a-rebus'. Explain to the children that a rebus is a message or story told with picture clues. Some young players may need to have some letters and numbers included in their message. Cryptic and entertaining messages can be sent using such visual clues, for example: *I see you think you can play football.*

NOW OR LATER

■ The children could work in groups and investigate established codes such as Morse code, semaphore, shorthand, and number codes such as postcodes and telephone numbers.

■ Messages sent in code can be made more interesting if they are written in invisible ink. There are pens available on the market that write in invisible ink which becomes visible if scribbled over with a second 'magic' pen. However, it is possible to make your own invisible ink. Messages written in lemon juice or milk will become invisible as they dry. To make the message reappear, heat the paper over a radiator. You can also write an invisible message by pressing hard on two sheets of paper, the top one should be dry but the bottom one should be wet. The wet sheet will reveal the message when it is held up to the light, but the indentation will disappear as it dries. To reveal the message, simply dampen the paper once more.

LIONS AND TIGERS

RESOURCES AND CLASSROOM ORGANIZATION

You will need to explain how this game is played and the various rules involved. You will need a copy of photocopiable page 20 for each child; photocopiable pages 21 and 22 (for 'Differentiation'); writing materials and paper.

This activity is best played in pairs, but can be played in groups or as a whole class.

OBJECTIVE

To enable children to: practise spelling, reasoning, deductive logic and hypothesizing.

WHAT TO DO

One player is chosen to start the game called 'Lions and tigers'. They choose a four-letter word and write it down but do not show it to the opponent. The word is, for example, *goat*. The players now use the game grid on photocopiable page 20.

The numbers across the top represent the four letters of the chosen mystery word. The lion and tiger are at the head of the scoring columns.

The player's opponent makes a first guess with the word *home* and writes it in the first row of the grid. Player I checks to see if there are any letters in the correct place. These would be 'lions'. There is one, the *o*, so they write *I* in the 'Lions' column. Then they check to see if there are any correct letters but in the wrong place. There are none.

Player 2 now makes a second guess, *trap*. This word has no correct letters in the right place so there are no lions. However, it does have two letters, *t* and *a*, in the wrong place, so the first player writes 2 in the 'Tigers' column. With the next guess, *toad*, the second player scores two lions, *o* and *a*, and one tiger, *t*.

The scores for this word would be written like this on the grid:

I	2	3	4	Lions	Tigers
H	O	M	E	I	0
T	R	A	P	0	2
T	O	A	D	2	I

And so the game continues with the second player making guesses based on the information in the 'Lions' and 'Tigers' columns, and the first player giving clues by indicating how close the suggestion is to the target word with scores in the 'Lions' and 'Tigers' columns. After they have played this game a few times the children will learn to pick words which keep the lion letters in the same position and have tiger letters in different positions.

DIFFERENTIATION

It is possible to make solving the puzzle easier for less able children by using a set of four symbols rather than the 'Lions' and 'Tigers' columns. This version is called 'Letter logic' and the principle of the game remains the same. One player has to guess the word written secretly by another by a series of guesses and deductions using the clues given. In this version a set of symbols is used to match the guess against the target word:

> ★ **Star:** the correct letter is earlier in the alphabet
> ▲ **Triangle:** the correct letter occurs later in the alphabet
> ✗ **Cross:** this is the correct letter in the wrong place
> ✔ **Tick:** this is the correct letter in the correct place

So if the first player writes *gave* as the target word, and the second player guesses *mine*, the first player would place his or her clues tin this way:

And if the second player then guessed *have*, the first player would mark his or her clues in this way:

A game grid for playing this 'Letter logic' version is on photocopiable page 22.

More able children may like to play the lions and tigers game with five-, six- or even seven-letter words. A game grid for playing with five-letter words is on photocopiable page 21.

NOW OR LATER

Children could play 'Lions and tigers' in small supportive groups using three-letter words. This is particularly suitable for less able children. You will need to draw up the three-letter grid and oversee the first few games.

ALPHABET ASSASSINATION

OBJECTIVE

To enable children to: develop spelling, vocabulary and dictionary skills.

RESOURCES AND CLASSROOM ORGANIZATION

You will need to explain how the game is played and the rules involved. You will need writing materials, lined paper and dictionaries.

The game is best played in pairs.

WHAT TO DO

The players should write all the letters of the alphabet down the left hand side of a page of lined paper, each letter on a different line. Player 1 writes a word that contains the letter *a*, for example *age*, and gives the paper to Player 2 who checks that the word is spelled correctly. If it is incorrectly spelled, Player 2 has a chance to write an *a* word. If it is correct Player 1 draws a circle around the letter *a* and Player 2 then writes a word containing *b*, such as *rub*. Player 1 checks it and if it is correct Player 2 draws a cross over the letter *b*. So the players score their circles or crosses if they write words that are correctly spelled containing the next letter of the alphabet.

The challenge occurs because players do not have to use only one letter from the alphabet sequence at a time. So Player 1 might now write *card*, gaining two points by using c and d. And Player 2 might respond with *effigy*, so acquiring three points for e, *f* and g. The three letters must follow in sequence in the alphabet, though they may be out of sequence in the word. So Player 1, following *effigy*, can gain two points by writing *Irish*, even though the next two letters in the alphabet *h* and *i* are out of sequence in the word.

The players continue, using a dictionary if they wish, until they have 'assassinated' the whole of the alphabet. The player with the most letters wins the round.

DIFFERENTIATION

The children could try to 'assassinate' the alphabet on their own. They could work through the alphabet trying to think of words that use multiple letters of the alphabet in the correct sequence, referring to a dictionary if they need to. The object of the game is to use up all the letters in only a few words, that is, to 'assassinate' the alphabet with the fewest possible shots. In this version the children play individually, competing against themselves, trying to better their own record.

NOW OR LATER

Encourage the children to play the solo version of 'Alphabet assassination' in their spare time. Set up a display board where the various efforts can be viewed, mistakes noted, and successes marvelled at!

SILENT *E* STORIES

OBJECTIVE
To enable children to: consolidate their knowledge of the silent e split digraph.

RESOURCES AND CLASSROOM ORGANIZATION

You will need to discuss the silent e with the children and remind them that in a word with a vowel, consonant then final e, the silent e on the end of the words changes the pronunciation of the previous vowel – that vowel 'says its name' (for example, *fin* and *fine*). You will need a board or flip chart on which to write a prepared list of paired words where the silent e can be added.

The children work individually.

WHAT TO DO

Show the children the list of paired words and ask them to invent a three or four line story that includes the pair of words. For example: *My pet goldfish had a droopy fin, but I took him to the vet and now it is fine.* The list of words you provide might include:

bit bite	hid hide	pet Pete	slid slide
can cane	hop hope	pin pine	strip stripe
cod code	kit kite	plan plane	tap tape
fin fine	mad made	rip ripe	Tim time
fir fire	man mane	rob robe	tub tube
Jan Jane	not note	Sam same	twin twine
hat hate	pal pale	scrap scrape	win wine

DIFFERENTIATION

Give pairs of children the task of working together to create a brief story with two, three or four pairs of silent e words, the exact number will depend on their ability.

NOW OR LATER

■ Go on a 'silent e' hunt. Ask the children to work in mixed ability groups to find as many 'silent e' words as they can from dictionaries, fiction and non-fiction books, magazines and so on, in a given time. Which team can make the longest list? Teams lose a point for words on the list that are incorrect!

■ When reading to the class, deliberately mispronounce silent e words and ask the children to correct you. For example: pronounce *chase* as *chas*, and *stage* as *stag*.

Name Date

Invented acronyms

■ Below is a list of well-known acronyms. Use a dictionary or other reference book to find out what the letters stand for.

UN ____________________

RAF ____________________

NATO ____________________

LASER ____________________

CAD ____________________

ERNIE ____________________

BA ____________________

SIS ____________________

AWOL ____________________

WHO ____________________

WYSIWYG ____________________

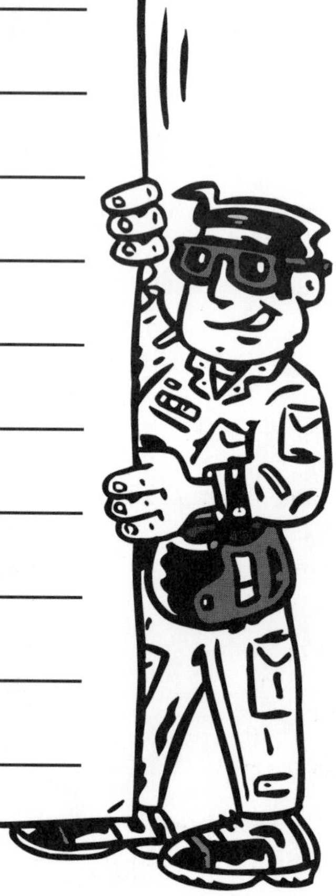

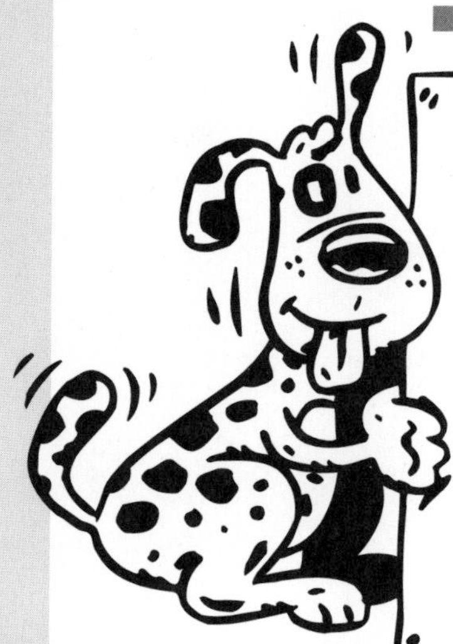

■ Now make up some acronyms of your own using these letters.

WIG ____________________

FAP ____________________

ERIC ____________________

SPOT ____________________

CATCH ____________________

Signing alphabet (American version)

G	N	U	
F	M	T	
E	L	S	Z
D	K	R	Y
C	J	Q	X
B	I	P	W
A	H	O	V

Lions and tigers (four-letter words)

1	2	3	4	Lions	Tigers

Lions and Tigers (Five-letter words)

1	2	3	4	5	Lions	Tigers

Photocopiables

Letter logic

	1	2	3	4
Guess 1				
Clues ★▲✗✔				
Guess 2				
Clues ★▲✗✔				
Guess 3				
Clues ★▲✗✔				
Guess 4				
Clues ★▲✗✔				
Guess 5				
Clues ★▲✗✔				
Guess 6				
Clues ★▲✗✔				
Guess 7				
Clues ★▲✗✔				
Guess 8				
Clues ★▲✗✔				
Guess 9				
Clues ★▲✗✔				
Guess 10				
Clues ★▲✗✔				

★ Star: the correct letter is earlier in the alphabet
▲ Triangle: the correct letter occurs later in the alphabet
✗ Cross: this is the correct letter in the wrong place
✔ Tick: this is the correct letter in the correct place

22

Section 2 GAMES WITH WORDS

The games in this section help children to build their vocabulary. They can be encouraged to widen their written vocabulary by a realization that they have more words to call on than they normally use. Some games will give the opportunity to put down on paper for the first time words that children have in their spoken vocabulary but are unsure how to spell and therefore would not normally write. It is easy to forget that children sometimes find new words awkward to handle. Within a game situation, playing with words can help overcome this lack of confidence. The section also introduces pupils to parts of speech. Teaching pupils about the functions of words in a sentence does not have to be an activity without enjoyment. In this section there are, for instance, fun activities which allow children to begin to understand the nature of verbs, adverbs and adjectives.

The activities in this section focus particularly on:
- encouraging fluency and confidence with vocabulary
- giving practice in context-free sight recognition of words
- encouraging an interest in word choices and nuances of meaning
- consolidating understanding of verbs, adverbs and adjectives, pronouns, and collective nouns
- introducing alliteration, puns and Spoonerisms
- introducing singular and plural forms of nouns, comparative and superlative forms of adjectives and adverbs, prefixes and suffixes.

HIDDEN WORDS

RESOURCES AND CLASSROOM ORGANIZATION

This activity requires a brief introduction to explain the concept of hidden words and the word game that the children will be playing. You will need a board or flip chart, a selection of fiction and non-fiction books, writing materials and paper.

The children should work in groups of four or five.

WHAT TO DO

Introduce this activity by talking to the whole class about words and explain that sometimes short words 'hide' longer ones within them. Write the following words on the board (each of them has at least one short word hiding inside it): *play*, *what*, *teacher*, *brother*, *birthday*.

Ask the children if they can identify the hidden words. Then divide the children into small groups, giving each group two or three fiction or non-fiction books. Each group should then turn to a page at random and search for other examples of hidden words. They should write down the longer word and underline the hidden word within it.

DIFFERENTIATION

More able children could try to find words with a minimum number of letters, such as four- or five-letter words, or adopt a scoring system where four-, five- or six-letter words count double. It will be necessary to find much longer words if this is to be feasible, for example: *navigate*, *archaeology*, *training*, *encourage*, *theatre*, *classical*, *permission*.

OBJECTIVE
To enable children to: look carefully at words, identifying syllables and/or letter strings that make separate words within words.

NOW OR LATER

■ There are some variations on this basic game that the children can play individually or in pairs. You could appoint a timekeeper and specify a time limit by which the children have to complete their investigations. Which child can find the most hidden words on a single page of their book in the specified time?

■ Ask the children to work individually or in pairs to find 20 longer words with hidden words inside them. They should then show their collection to another child or pair to see if they can pick out the hidden words.

■ The children could play individually, choosing a word from a collection to see how many new words they can generate from its letters. In this version, the children can rearrange the letters in any order, but they must not use a letter more times than it appears in the original. Here are some words that the children could use for this game:

photography	accidental	thoughtful	international	multiplication
atmosphere	investment	performance	calculators	intelligent
elementary	flamboyant	contaminate	blindfold	flabbergasted
literature	restaurant	opportunity	sentimental	wilderness

VERB DETECTIVE

OBJECTIVES
To enable children to:
■ consolidate their understanding of verbs
■ develop their questioning skills.

RESOURCES AND CLASSROOM ORGANIZATION

Before playing this game some children may need a brief reminder about what a verb is and how verbs are used in different sentences.

This game can be played in small groups or by the whole class. You will need to supervise as the game is played.

WHAT TO DO

One player should be chosen to be the verb detective and is sent out of the room. The other players have to choose a mystery verb, such as *cough*, *draw* or *drive*. The verb detective is invited back into the room to discover the mystery verb. He or she must do this by going around the group asking questions in which the unknown verb is replaced by the words *Sherlock Holmes*. For example the verb detective might ask:

■ Can animals Sherlock Holmes?
■ Where is the best place to Sherlock Holmes?
■ Have you Sherlock Holmesed today?
■ Do you need any special equipment to Sherlock Holmes?

The verb detective can make a guess at the mystery verb at any time, and if the guess is wrong just keep on asking questions. Once the mystery verb is discovered, a new verb detective is chosen, and the group secretly chooses another mystery verb.

DIFFERENTIATION

There are different strategies that can be applied to this game to make it easier. It is better, for example, if the children answering the question are encouraged not to give just yes or no answers, but to add some details that might help the detective. For example, if the verb is *draw* and the detective asks if you need any special equipment, then the answering player might say, *Actually yes, a pencil or crayon, and paper would come in handy.* And if the verb detective has trouble guessing the mystery verb, then players are allowed to help by suggesting questions that might be asked. For example: *Why don't you ask me if everyone in this room has done it earlier today?* or *Why don't you ask me how long it takes to Sherlock Holmes?*

NOW OR LATER
Brainstorm questions that might be asked before the game begins. Players might write these down and have them to hand ready for when they become the verb detectives.

GUESS THE ADVERB

RESOURCES AND CLASSROOM ORGANIZATION
This game requires an introduction and some preparation. You will need to prepare a list of verbs and adverbs for the children to use in the game. You will also need a board or flip chart.

The children should play this game as a whole class and will need enough space for them to sit in a circle. You will need to supervise this activity.

OBJECTIVE
To enable children to: consolidate their understanding of verbs and adverbs.

WHAT TO DO
Introduce the game by reminding the class what verbs and adverbs are and how they can be identified in a sentence. You could write one or two example sentences on the board and ask individual children to come out and underline the verbs and adverbs.

Then explain how to play the game. Give one player, or several players, a list of verbs to read, such as *run*, *cough* and *whisper* and ask them to go out of earshot and choose one. Meanwhile, give the rest of the class an adverb such as *quietly*, *excitedly* or *calmly*. The other players return and give the rest of the class their chosen verb. The rest of the class must act out the verb that they have been given in the manner of the adverb. For example: *He ran excitedly, She coughed quietly* or *He whispered calmly*. Based upon what they see, the first group must try to guess the adverb. If they are wrong, they choose another verb from their list and try again.

DIFFERENTIATION
More able children can be asked to think of their own verbs rather than be given a list. Confident children could take the part of the teacher and provide the adverb for the class to act.

Less able children could play the game in pairs or small groups. You could give one child a card on which you have written a simple sentence such as *She coughed quietly*. They then act out the sentence while the other children guess both the verb and the adverb. When they have guessed correctly the children should write the sentence down.

NOW OR LATER
Once the children are confident about playing this game, they could write their own lists of verbs and adverbs and play the game in small groups. Skimming through fiction books may help them to identify some interesting adverbs.

WORD WALLS

OBJECTIVES

To enable children to:
■ become interested in word choices and meanings
■ extend their vocabulary.

RESOURCES AND CLASSROOM ORGANIZATION

An introduction is required, including an explanation of how to fill in photocopiable page 38. You will need a reading text – a short story, a poem or a section of a novel – and a copy of photocopiable page 38 for each child and writing materials.

The children could work in pairs, small groups or together as a whole class.

WHAT TO DO

Show the children photocopiable page 38 and explain that, during or after reading a text, they could begin to fill in a word wall by identifying particularly interesting or significant words from the text. For example, you could say: *Write down any adjectives you hear while I am reading* or: *Fill in the word wall with any words that you think are there to create a feeling of sadness* or simply: *Write down any words you hear which you think are longer than six letters.*

At the end of the session you could compare the children's different selections from the same text, identifying opposites to words recorded on the wall.

Ask the children to identify their own categories for a word wall.

DIFFERENTIATION

The categories that the children are asked to use to complete a word wall can be more or less difficult depending on their abilities. At the simplest level the instruction could be: *Write down any words that interest you.* More challenging would be instructions such as: *Write down any adverbs or conjunctions or pronouns you hear as I read* or: *Write down on the wall any words that you think the author has used to try to persuade.*

NOW OR LATER

■ Those children who are used to focusing on the vocabulary in texts using word walls will be able to focus on the language of a text in other ways. Ask them, for example, to quote a phrase from their current reading book that particularly strikes them as having interesting language. Or they could collect a range of first lines to stories from books in the classroom and discuss how these work.

■ Ask the children to build a word wall from their current story book which highlights the language the author is using to describe the behaviour, feelings, attitudes and personality of a character in that book.

■ Select some of the children's own writing to reflect on through a word wall. Make enlarged copies, perhaps laminated, of their word walls and put them on display.

READING RACES

OBJECTIVES

To enable children to:
■ practise skim-reading
■ learn different parts of speech
■ extend their vocabulary.

RESOURCES AND CLASSROOM ORGANIZATION

This activity comprises several different versions of what is one basic game idea. Each version requires a little preparation before it can be played. For 'Preposition racing' you will need to prepare a list of prepositions for the children to use. For 'Auxiliary verb racing' you will need to prepare a list of auxiliary verbs. For each version you will need to remind the children what is meant by each of the parts of speech and how they are used in sentences. You will also be needed to score each game.

You will need a selection of fiction books with roughly equal amounts of print, writing materials, tracing paper, acetates or writing paper.

These games can have any number of players from two to the whole class.

WHAT TO DO

There are a variety of versions of this game, which requires players to skim-read a book and to mark parts of speech in the passage that they are reading. This might be done by using sheets of tracing paper or acetates, or simply by writing down page and line numbers of the 'finds' on paper.

'Preposition racing': the players are given a list of prepositions, such as *in, out, down, up, with, through, over, behind*. Then, within a set time, they must identify and write down the references (page number and line) for as many of these as they can in the book they have in front of them. The player who claims to have found the most identifications has their answers checked by you or an appointed referee and, if the identifications are correct is declared the winner. If there are mistakes the answers of the player with the second highest list of identifications are checked, until a winner is agreed.

'Auxiliary verb racing': this game is played in the same way as 'Preposition racing', except that the list players are given is now a list of auxiliary verbs, such as *will, have, do, be, shall, are*.

'Conjunction racing': this game is played in a similar way to the two above except that it is possible to extend the complexity of the activity by changing the scoring. For example, each player scores:
- one point for a conjunction joining two words (*neither boys **nor** girls*)
- two points for a conjunction joining two phrases (*all the king's horses **and** all the king's men*)
- three points for a conjunction joining two clauses (*the man was angry **because** he had forgotten his car keys*).

DIFFERENTIATION

For those children who need a greater challenge, the parts of speech they are asked to identify could be extended. For example, the children could be asked to identify proper noun phrases, such as: *Harry's sorting hat, the gluttonous Augustus Gloop* or *the skyscrapers of New York*.

NOW OR LATER

- Cut out short strips of card or paper. Write on them the clauses identified in the game 'Conjunction racing'. Try mixing up the clauses from the different sentences, adding conjunctions and changing word endings for agreement, to make complex sentences and see what kind of nonsense you can create.
- Play 'Word hunt racing', a simple game in which the children have to find words that have a given feature by skim-reading through a reading book. For example, they could look for a word that has double letters, a word that has three or more vowels or a word that is a proper noun. The children should start the game with a closed book and on the command *Go*, open the book and skim-read to find the word with the feature that is the focus for that round. The first player to find such a word shouts it out and scores one point. Players then have to shut their books, and the next round starts with the same word type, or with a new feature to be hunted down.

FICTIONARY

OBJECTIVES

To enable children to:
- practise dictionary skills
- develop their vocabulary
- appreciate nuances of meaning.

RESOURCES AND CLASSROOM ORGANIZATION

This activity requires an introduction to ensure that the children understand how to use a dictionary. You will need an adult dictionary to use during your introduction, good, general-purpose adult dictionaries, writing materials, slips of paper or cards and a clipboard or book.

This game should be played in groups of between three and ten.

WHAT TO DO

Before introducing the game, talk to the class about dictionaries, how they are used and the way in which they explain or define words. Show the children an adult dictionary and ask them to suggest two or three words that you could look up. Read out the definitions and talk to the children about the way in which the definitions are presented, and the style and format of the dictionary.

Then explain how the game is played. Divide the children into groups or teams of three to ten and choose one child from each group to be the 'fictionarian'. They should open the dictionary at random and look for a word that they think none of the rest of the group will know. For example, the word *lave* could be picked. The fictionarian then spells the word to the rest of the group who write it down on a card. Each member of the group now makes up a dictionary definition of the word and writes it down making sure no one else sees it. They also write their name. The fictionarian should write two definitions, one they have made up, for example, *lave: a ditch running alongside a field*, and the other the main definition from the dictionary – *lave: to wash or bathe*.

The fictionarian should then collect all the definitions, including their own, number them consecutively, and shuffle them well. They should conceal the definitions behind a book or clipboard and read out each one along with its number, without giving any clue as to which is correct. The other players have to consider which definition seems the most convincing and write down its number.

The fictionarian then calls out the numbers again and the rest of the group put their hands up when the fictionarian comes to the number they have chosen. The fictionarian counts the number of hands and writes it on the definition card. They now read out the definitions again, naming the author of each fake definition (including their own). The number of people who chose the fake definition becomes that players score. Players who chose the correct definition score two extra points.

For the next round, the chance to be fictionarian passes to another player and the game continues until everyone in the group has had a chance to be the fictionarian.

DIFFERENTIATION

A simplified version of this game could be played orally with less able children. Choose a word from the dictionary and make up three or four fake definitions. (It is not too difficult to do this ad lib.) Slowly tell the class the fake definitions, slipping in the correct definition at some point. Then ask the children to guess which was the correct definition and then ask them to check their dictionaries to see who was right.

NOW OR LATER

This game can be played competitively between small groups of the same number. Each group together is asked to find in their dictionary a word that is so obscure that other groups will not know its meaning. Then each player in the group writes a short definition of the word, but only one player writes the correct meaning – the others are made up. Each player now reads out the definition they have to the opposing group who have to guess which player is giving the correct definition and which are bluffing. If the team guess correctly they score one point and the play is reversed. Ingenuity and good acting are required in order to make the false definitions seem at least as plausible as the true one.

SINGULAR AND PLURAL

RESOURCES AND CLASSROOM ORGANIZATION

This activity requires an introduction to remind the children of the spelling rules of singular and plural nouns. You will need a board or flip chart, writing materials, A4 paper and dictionaries.

This game can be played by any number of children from two to the whole class.

WHAT TO DO

Introduce this activity by explaining or revising the spelling rules of singular and plural nouns. Show the children some examples on the board.

This game is best played as a race. Give each child a sheet of A4 paper, which they should fold in half lengthways, or draw a line down the centre of, to form two columns. On one column they should write the heading *Singular* and on the other *Plural*. Now nominate an 'environment' such as *the classroom, the library, the playground, the UK* or *the Earth*. Give the children a set time in which to list as many items as they can think of for each column. For example, if the chosen environment were the UK, then *River Thames* would go in the *Singular* column, but the word *field* would be written in the *Plural* column, and so on. When the time limit is reached the children swap papers to add the number of words in each column.

They should refer to the you as the referee, or take a vote amongst the other players, if they are unsure about the validity of any entry in either column.

Announce a 'singular winner' and a 'plural winner'.

OBJECTIVES

To enable children to:
■ consolidate their understanding of singular and plural
■ learn the spelling of plural nouns.

DIFFERENTIATION

This game can be made more difficult by an insistence that the items written in each column must be spelled correctly to 'score'. You may need to remind the children of the spelling rules for common plurals. (For example: *-y* to *-ies* in the plural, as in *story/-ies*.) A dictionary should to be available for all the children to use.

NOW OR LATER

Using the singular and plural nouns written in the course of the game, invent rules for the players to use in writing sentences using singulars and plurals. For example: *Write a sentence with one singular noun and two plural nouns* or: *Write a sentence with two plural nouns and no singular nouns.*

COMPARATIVE AND SUPERLATIVE

OBJECTIVE

To enable children to: learn the comparative and superlative forms of adjectives.

RESOURCES AND CLASSROOM ORGANIZATION

This activity requires an introduction to explain how the comparative and superlative forms of adjectives are used both in written and spoken English. Prepare an illustrated list of examples on a board or flip chart before the session.

The children will need enough room to sit in a circle in small groups or as a whole class. You will need to supervise the game.

WHAT TO DO

Show the children your illustrated list of adjectives. You could write, for example: *fat, fatter, fattest* and illustrate this with drawings of a cat or: *big, bigger, biggest* and illustrate this with pictures of a car. Then show the children three pictures of the same object at different sizes with the comparatives and superlatives covered up. For example: a building (*tall, taller, tallest*) or: a person with a long nose (*long, longer, longest*). Ask different children to come out and point to a picture and say the comparative or superlative form. Then reveal the words to see if they are correct.

When the children have understood this concept, divide them into groups if you wish and ask each group to sit in a circle. The first player should make up a fib and tell it to the others, for example: *I'm small – as small as a mouse*. The next player is the 'comparative' fibber and has to improve on the first fib. So he or she could say: *I'm smaller – as small as an ant*. Then the third player who is the 'superlative' fibber has to produce the most exaggerated fib, for example: *I'm the smallest – as small as an atom*. Then the next player around the circle must start with a new fib.

You might want to start the game off by suggesting words that could be used to invent fibs. For example:

> *Strong, stronger, strongest*   *Clean, cleaner, cleanest*
> *Rich, richer, richest*   *Heavy, heavier, heaviest*

DIFFERENTIATION

Children of all abilities could collect comparative and superlative adjectives and draw cartoons illustrating the words. They might for example draw three pictures of monsters illustrating *ugly, uglier, ugliest*.

NOW OR LATER

This game can be played competitively, with players given an agreed amount of time to invent their fib. If a player finds themselves tongue-tied and unable to find a fib in the agreed time they are 'out'. Players continue to drop out until just one player is left as the winner.

HAPPY PRONOUN FAMILIES

RESOURCES AND CLASSROOM ORGANIZATION

This activity requires a brief introduction to explain the term 'personal pronoun' and the word game that the children will be playing. You will need to make a set of personal pronoun playing cards. These should be cards containing six personal pronoun families, with four members of each family (see the examples below).

This game can be played in groups of four or five.

> I, me, mine, myself   He, him, his, himself   We, us, our, ourselves
> You, your, yours, yourself   She, her, hers, herself   They, them, their, themselves

WHAT TO DO

This game is played in the same way as 'Happy families' – that is to say, the set of personal pronoun cards is dealt to the players who then, in turn, ask each other if they have a member of the family they are trying to collect. In order that all the players are always involved, the game should stop when the first player declares that they have collected a whole personal pronoun family and lays them down. A new game can then commence.

DIFFERENTIATION

The game can be played using different sets of cards. For example, the children could make a pack of cards that feature families of words featuring:

■ two, three, four, five and six syllables
■ the same vowel phoneme – *oo, ee, ea, ie, oa, ai*
■ the same word ending – *tion, ing, er, ent, y, ful*
■ the same part of speech – vowel, adverb, noun, preposition, adjective, conjunction
■ synonyms – for example for *walk, said* or *eat*.

NOW OR LATER

One way to encourage the children to think about word families is to draw a word web. For example, if you wanted to discuss how the context of a word can affect its meaning then you might draw a word web for the variety of lexical sets in which the word *eye* appears:

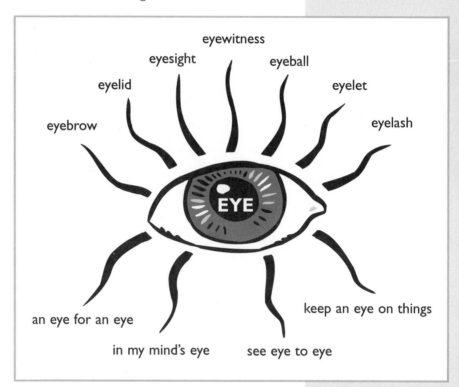

A MASH OF POTATOES

RESOURCES AND CLASSROOM ORGANIZATION

This activity requires a brief introduction to explain the concept of collective nouns and the word game that the children will be playing. You will need a board or flip chart and poster-size sheets of paper and writing materials.

This game should be played by three groups of equal number.

WHAT TO DO

Talk to the children about nouns and ask them to give you some examples. Then introduce and explain the term 'collective noun' and, using some of the children's suggestions of nouns, write the collective noun for them on the board. Then tell the children that in this game they are going to make up some unusual collective nouns of their own.

Divide the children into three equal teams. Each team should be given a large sheet of paper on which they draw three columns with the headings *People, Animals* and *Objects.* The teams now brainstorm plural nouns that might fit into the three columns. They write them into the columns leaving a space in front of each one for the collective noun to be added in later.

A limit should be placed on the number of nouns required, or a time limit given; both should be based on the abilities of the children. When the teams are ready they

OBJECTIVES

To enable children to:
■ learn about collective nouns
■ develop an understanding of how to organize information in sets.

should exchange lists. Now all three teams have to think up collective nouns that might be used for each item in the list they have been given – the more unusual, but apt, the better. For example:

People	Animals	Objects
an aerial of acrobats	*an establishment of elephants*	*a mash of potatoes*
a baggage of bullies	*a flutter of butterflies*	*a democracy of desks*
a skid of skiers	*a howling of dogs*	*a transparency of windows*

When they have finished, or time is up, one player from each team should read out their ideas. With each list there will be one of the three teams that has not contributed. This team must vote on each idea for a collective noun in that list. When all three teams have voted on the list they made no contribution to, the scores are added together to determine the winning team.

DIFFERENTIATION

Children could use reference books to discover the conventional collective nouns for various groups of animals, objects or people. Discuss how these compare with the invented ones.

NOW OR LATER

Individuals might play this game for their own amusement. Build a class collection by placing a large sheet of plain paper on the wall in the classroom and ask the children to invent collective nouns in spare moments and write them on the poster, perhaps with an illustration.

LIST CRAZY

OBJECTIVE
To enable children to: acquire fluency and confidence with vocabulary.

RESOURCES AND CLASSROOM ORGANIZATION
You will need paper, writing materials and dictionaries (optional).
   This is a simple, list-building game for any number of players from two to the whole class.

WHAT TO DO
Explain to the children that you want them to think of words that have something in common. For example they might build lists of:

- words with double letters (*tunnel*, *middle*, *happy*)
- words with more than two vowels (*station*, *please*, *house*)
- words that contain either *x* or *z* (*oxygen*, *ozone*, *zoo*, *wax*)
- words that have three or more syllables (*kangaroo*, *performance*, *mathematician*).

You could decide on the feature to be listed, or players could write ideas on a slip of paper, put them in a container and draw one out. Set a time limit, such as ten minutes, and allow the players to list as many words with the common feature as they can in the time. When time is up, players swap lists to check that the words follow the rule for that round and are spelled correctly. Dictionaries could be used for checking – incorrect spelling does not count. The winner is the player with the longest list.

DIFFERENTIATION
This game can be played at any level according to the ability of the players. A category such as *pairs of homophones* might be

32

chosen for very able children. Less able children could play the game in pairs for support and be asked to build lists in simpler categories.

NOW OR LATER

Lists can make an effective simple poetic form, and a wide variety of lists can be a good starting point – lists of similes or collective nouns, or comparative lists. Possible titles could include: 'A Rich Man or Poor Man's Shopping List', 'Things I Like', or 'Reasons to be Cheerful'.

ALLITERATIVE NAMES

RESOURCES AND CLASSROOM ORGANIZATION

This activity requires an introduction to explain the term 'alliteration'. You should also prepare a short list of examples on a board or flip chart to amplify your introduction.

This activity is for the whole class sitting in a circle.

OBJECTIVES

To enable children to:
■ learn about alliteration
■ consolidate their understanding of adjectives.

WHAT TO DO

Begin by explaining that alliteration is when two or more words close to each other begin with the same first sound or letter. You will also need to explain the nature of the adjective–noun connection. Show the children the list that you have prepared on the board. You could list, for example, names of racehorses as many are given alliterative names: Silver Streak, Red Rum, Moon Mariner. Ask the children if they can suggest some other names and add these to your list.

Then ask one child to describe themselves using a word that starts with the same first letter as their first name, such as *Happy Hanif, Fearless Fred* or *Sweet Susan*. The next child does the same, and so on around the circle. On the next round each person chooses an alliterative name, not for themselves, but for the person to their left. So Helen could call Fred *Famous Fred*, and Fred could call Susan, *Sunshine Susan*. (It is important that you firmly rule out insults before the game starts. Nothing like *Fat Fred* should be allowed!) The game might be repeated using surnames.

DIFFERENTIATION

There are a number of variations on this game, but some are beyond the capabilities of all but the most able children. For example, the game could be made competitive by disqualifying children if they hesitate for longer than a certain number of seconds, so that as each round progresses, and players have to choose a different alliterative name on each round, the number of players gradually diminishes. Similarly, a rule might be introduced which prohibits players from repeating an adjective that has been previously used in that round.

Less able children could be given pictures of wild or domestic animals and asked to make up suitable alliterative names for them. For example: *Roderick the Rabbit* and *Teresa the Tiger*. They could do the same with well-known pop stars or sportsmen. For extra support you could also give them a list of appropriate adjectives from which to choose, such as *Beautiful Britney, Rowdy Robbie, Marvellous Michael* and *Dashing David*.

NOW OR LATER

As a variation, this activity can be played as a memory game. It is actually a version of 'I'm going on a picnic', but it is good to play with a group who do not know each other, since it can be used as a way of everyone remembering each other's names. Once one person has said their alliterative name, the next person must say that alliterative name as well as their own, and then the next must say the two previous names before their own, and so on around the circle, with each person saying all those before their own.

BEGINNINGS AND ENDINGS

OBJECTIVES

To enable children to:
■ improve spelling by increasing understanding of prefixes and suffixes
■ practise dictionary skills.

RESOURCES AND CLASSROOM ORGANIZATION

This activity requires a brief introduction to explain or remind children about prefixes and suffixes. Prepare a list of words on a board or flip chart to which you can add prefixes and suffixes during your introduction. You will need dice, a copy of photocopiable page 39 for each group, writing materials and an adult dictionary.

This game is best played in small groups.

WHAT TO DO

Introduce this game by explaining to the class what prefixes and suffixes are and how they are used for different words, changing their meanings. Then show the children your list of example words on the board and to some of these add either a prefix or suffix as appropriate. Then ask individual children to come out and add either a prefix or a suffix to the remaining words.

Divide the children into groups. Then explain how the game is played. One player in each group is elected Prime Minister for the first round. The Prime Minister throws the dice three times to start the game.

The first number determines which of the tables on photocopiable page 39 will be used. The second throw determines which prefix or suffix in that table is the focus for the round. The third throw determines how many words the players (including the Prime Minister) must find. Each word must start with the given prefix or end with the given suffix.

The children should use a dictionary to help them or to check their spellings. When one pair or group has written the right number of words one player should call out 'elected'. All the other players must immediately put down their pencils. The Prime Minister then throws the dice again and this number determines how many points each of the words is worth. The children should work in pairs to check spellings and calculate scores. The player with the highest score in the round is elected to be the Prime Minister for the next round. Players accumulate scores for each round, and the winner, and Prime Minister for the day, is the player with the highest total at the end of the game.

DIFFERENTIATION

The children could write their own prefix and suffix tables, rather than be given the photocopiable sheet, or add to those given. More able children could work out the meanings for the prefixes from the words collected. For example: pre – before; ad – towards, against; con – together, and so on.

NOW OR LATER

Play the game in the same format but make tables that contain other parts of words. For example, tables containing particular phonemes that are being taught at the time, or particular common spelling patterns such as -ious, or -iable.

SPOONERISMS

RESOURCES AND CLASSROOM ORGANIZATION

This activity requires an introduction and some preparation. You will need to prepare some examples of Spoonerisms prior to the session to discuss with the class during your introduction. You will also need a board or flip chart, writing materials and paper.

Children work as a whole class then individually.

WHAT TO DO

Explain to the class that Spoonerisms occur when the initial sounds of spoken words are transposed, either individual letters, letter clusters, or syllables. They are named after the Reverend William Spooner (1844–1930), an Oxford scholar who was renowned for this form of word mix-up. One of the most famous of Spooner's errors was: *Sir, you have deliberately tasted two whole worms* instead of *Sir, you have deliberately wasted two whole terms.*

Show the children one or two Spoonerisms that you have prepared on the board and ask the class to translate them back into sensible sentences. For example:

> *Have you crushed my bat?*
> (Have you brushed my cat?)
>
> *You have hissed your mystery lesson.*
> (You have missed your history lesson.)

Now ask the children to work individually to invent and write down a Spoonerism. After a short while choose a few children to read out what they have written and then write their Spoonerisms on the board for the class to 'solve'.

DIFFERENTIATION

More able children will be able to devise small dramatic scenes for their Spoonerisms. Suggest a scenario, such as two people meeting for the first time at a party, a shop assistant and customer, a waiter and restaurant guest, a football player and a referee or a TV repairman and a householder. Ask pairs of children to devise a conversation, taking on the roles defined, but inventing Spoonerisms as the discussion progresses. Each pair could make a record of their invented dialogue to read back to the class, or pairs might take it in turns to record their conversation on a tape-recorder.

Written Spoonerisms do not indicate the amusement as well as spoken versions can, but an example might be:

> **Woman in restaurant:** Waiter, there's a sly in my foup.
> **Waiter:** I'm morry, sadam, there is nothing I can do. That's the meat!
> **Woman:** But I only veat egetables.
> **Waiter:** Okay, madam. I'll metch the fanager.

NOW OR LATER

You might display the best Spoonerisms around the classroom and ask the children to vote for their favourite examples.

OBJECTIVES

To enable children to:
■ be aware of the onset in words
■ understand Spoonerisms.

SQUEEZED WORDS

RESOURCES AND CLASSROOM ORGANIZATION

This game requires a brief introduction to explain what the children have to do. You will need a board or flip chart, writing materials and paper.

This game should be played by two teams.

WHAT TO DO

Introduce the activity by explaining to the children that 'squeezed' words are made up of parts of two other words 'squashed' together. For example: *brunch* is *breakfast* and *lunch*. The computer term *bits* is *binary* and *digits* squeezed together. Explain the famous example of the writer Lewis Carroll making up his own squeezed words such as *mimsy* (perhaps *miserable* and *flimsy*).

Divide the children into two teams. Each team should invent as many squeezed words as they can within a given time period. The teams should be given categories for these new squeezed words. For example:

> *New creatures* – a *tigon* might be a cross between a lion and tiger.
> *New games* – *skipscotch* might be a game which involves skipping down a hopscotch path.
> *New gadgets* – a *knork* is a fork with a knife edge on one side.
> *New food* – scientists have invented a chocolate flavoured banana, a *chocana*.

Each team should pick a category and compile a list of things that belong in that category. Then they should choose a pair of these words and see if they can make up a new word by 'squeezing' them together; the first part of one word with the last part of the other. When the teams have thought of a number of new creations they should write them down and pass them over to the other team who have to guess what these new words might mean.

DIFFERENTIATION

Teams of confident children might be asked to write dictionary definitions of their new squeezed words, place them in alphabetical order in a notebook and create a squeezed word dictionary.

NOW OR LATER

Ask the teams to draw representations of their new words on separate pieces of paper. When both teams have thought up their squeezed words and drawn pictures, they could exchange papers and have fun trying to match up the words and pictures.

TERRIFIC TITLES

RESOURCES AND CLASSROOM ORGANIZATION

This activity will require a brief introduction. You will need writing materials and paper.

Children could work individually, in groups or together as a whole class.

OBJECTIVES
To enable children to:
■ appreciate the fun of language
■ gain an understanding of puns.

WHAT TO DO

Explain to the children that a pun is a play on words which makes a sort of joke. Provide one or two examples to help the children to understand, such as: *Deciding where to bury him was a grave concern.*

Then tell the children that the aim of the game is to invent imaginary book titles and authors' names that together make punning jokes. The children's book titles could include:
- *The Millionaire* by Ivor Mint
- *Get Rich Quick* by Robin Banks
- *A Trip to the Dentist* by Phil McAvity
- *Losing Weight* by LE Fant
- *Bird Watching* by Freda Parrot
- *Toddler Games* by Ben D Toy
- *It's an Upside Down World* by Honor Head
- *The Shape of Things to Come* by Polly Gone.

The children could have double the fun – thinking up their own titles and then hearing everyone else's at the end of the session.

DIFFERENTIATION

There are a number of variations of this activity that should extend children's expertise with puns. You could, for example, ask the children to make up family joke names. Perhaps they could write a party guest list inviting as many joke families as possible. They might wish to invite:
- Mr and Mrs Cumber and their son Hugh
- Mr and Mrs Croscope, the scientists, and their son Mike, and Mike's spotlessly clean relation, Auntie Septic
- recent lottery winners Mr and Mrs Fortune and their sad daughter, Miss Fortune
- flushed with success, Mr and Mrs Blood-Vessel and their florid-faced son Buster
- pride of the party, Mr and Mrs Lion and their noisy son Rory.

The children could then try to match joke names to an occupation. For example:
- Polly Tician is an MP.
- Electra Fide repairs televisions.
- Cliff Hanger is a crime writer.
- Will Steel is a burglar.
- Chip Board is a DIY expert.
- Rose Petal is a florist.

Ask the children to write a phrase or short sentence to describe a character with an amusing name, for instance:
- Sandy Beech is always on holiday.
- Miss Sing Toh has now stopped mowing lawns for a living.
- Michael Moon would only come out at night.
- Terry Dactyl is mad about dinosaurs.

NOW OR LATER

If the class can invent enough 'terrific titles' you could cover a set of books with plain paper jackets, ask the children to write and illustrate the covers, and make a display shelf of books by joke authors.

Word wall

Beginnings and endings

1

1	2	3	4	5	6
ab (absent)	**ad** (advance)	**bi** (bicycle)	**con** (contrary)	**de** (defeat)	**ex** (exit)

2

1	2	3	4	5	6
in (injection)	**pre** (present)	**pro** (project)	**sub** (subway)	**super** (superman)	**tele** (television)

3

1	2	3	4	5	6
trans (transmit)	**tri** (triangle)	**dis** (disinfect)	**re** (reinforce)	**ob** (obtain)	**un** (unfit)

4

1	2	3	4	5	6
-or (director)	**-ite** (opposite)	**-ment** (merriment)	**-ty** (plenty)	**-ing** (helping)	**-tion** (station)

5

1	2	3	4	5	6
auto	**semi**	**ultra**	**per**	**inter**	**im**

6

1	2	3	4	5	6
anti	**ante**	**non**	**-ly**	**-ty**	**-ic**

GAMES WITH SENTENCES

Many of the activities in this section ask children to explore sentence construction. Some games, if supported by discussion, will draw attention to the structural properties that sentences have in common. You might, for example, following one of the games, lead a discussion towards the fact that verbs function as the nucleus of a sentence, and explain how children can check for themselves the presence of verbs in sentences in their own writing. Other games will, for instance, provide an experience of the place of adverbs and adjectives in sentences. An understanding of descriptive technical language is not needed to enjoy the games, but can be introduced whenever you judge it appropriate.

The games in this section focus particularly on:
- building sentence-making skills and understanding of a single complete sentence
- consolidating understanding of different sentence types, such as statements and questions
- building understanding of proverbs and similes
- practising accurate reading and the use of context cues.

WHY, WHAT, WHO, WHERE, HOW?

OBJECTIVES

To enable children to:
- understand the difference between questions and statements
- practise organized reasoning.

RESOURCES AND CLASSROOM ORGANIZATION

You will need two small pieces of paper or card for each child and writing materials.

This is a large group or whole class activity.

WHAT TO DO

Introduce this activity by discussing different questions and answers with the whole class. Ensure that the children understand what a sentence statement is.

Give out the pieces of paper to each child. Then ask all the children to write a question to which they know the answer on one piece. This question might be: *What is the name of the largest lake in England?* or *Who wrote 'Charlie and the Chocolate Factory'?* or *Where does the headteacher do her food shopping?* On the second piece of paper the children should write a full sentence statement (not a word, or phrase) in answer to that question. For example: *Lake Windermere is the largest lake in England,* or *Roald Dahl wrote 'Charlie and the Chocolate Factory'* or *The headteacher does her food shopping in Asda.*

Collect all the questions and answer statements, keeping them in separate piles. Mix up the questions and give them out again, one to each child. Then do the same with the answers. If someone is given their original question or answer, ask them to exchange. Now each child in turn should read out the question and answer on the pieces of paper they have just been given.

The mismatches often give rise to quite surreal but amusing answers. Everyone should listen carefully to see if they can identify the person who has the correct answer to the question on their

piece of paper. When everyone has read out their question and answer, each child should read out their question again and then try to identify who has the correct answer.

DIFFERENTIATION

This is a game that can be played by children of all abilities and without a great deal of teacher supervision. Divide the children into large mixed-ability groups, and they can then play the game on their own. Remind them that they must write full sentences for the questions and answers.

NOW OR LATER

This game might also be played to consolidate learning of a particular topic. For example, if the children are studying a particular historical period, you could prepare a set of questions and answers based upon the study topic, mix them up and give them out to the groups to match up using the same game format. Similarly, the game can be played with number facts.

SATISFACTORY SENTENCES

RESOURCES AND CLASSROOM ORGANIZATION

This is a simple oral word game, requiring a short introduction. You may want to use a board or flip chart for examples.

The game can be played by the whole class or in large groups.

WHAT TO DO

Introduce the activity by explaining to the class how the game is played. The children have to work together to keep a single sentence growing by adding words to it.

One child begins the game by saying a word that could come at the beginning of a sentence. For example: *Once…* That child then points to another player, Player 2, who has to say the next word in what will be a class- or group-generated sentence. For example: *Once when…* Player 2 now points to Player 3 to choose a word, for example, *I*, and so on. The game continues until the current player cannot think of a word that will carry the sentence on. He or she should then decide that a satisfactory sentence has been formed and then simply shout *And so they lived happily ever after!* This player then chooses who will start the next game.

DIFFERENTIATION

Less able children could be supported by having a list of connectives written on a board or flip chart, for example: *and, because, which, that.*

An alphabetical version of this game can be played by more able children. The rules are that each player adds a word starting with the next letter of the alphabet to make a coherent sentence. This version of the game can prove very challenging. For example: *A brown cat dashed eagerly forward.*

NOW OR LATER

There are several different versions of 'Satisfactory sentences', which have different levels of difficulty:

■ The oral game outlined above can be played competitively in a written version. Divide the children into small teams and ask each one to work together to write down the longest sentence that they can think up. A time limit should be placed on this part of the game. When time is up, the teams should then nominate one child to read out their sentence. The teams should then compare results. You might play three or four rounds with the teams and give a time limit for each round.

■ Alternatively, if you wish to play the game with the whole class, then each team member could write his or her contribution to the 'satisfactory sentence' on the board or flip chart rather than on paper so that everyone can see. With this option the first player in each team should run to the board and write his or her word, and then run back to 'tag' the second player who writes the second word, and so on until the team completes their 'satisfactory sentence'. The first team to finish wins. The challenge can be increased by placing a minimum number of words needed before the team is allowed to complete the sentence, so that each team member has to make two or three contributions to the gradually emerging long sentence before it can be ended.

■ One version requires a set of alphabet cards. This can be played in small groups. Place the shuffled pack of cards face down in the centre of the table. The first player turns over a card and says a word beginning with the letter turned up. The next

player turns up a card and says a word that starts with the letter revealed, but which also follows the first word and helps to build a sentence. Each player adds a word to the sentence in turn. At any point, a player can shout *Full stop* if they think their word finishes the sentence. Players can pass if they cannot think of a suitable word, but they should be encouraged to use their ingenuity to find a word each time.

■ Another version can be played with the whole class. Write a sentence, any sentence, on the board or flip chart. Now ask the class to use the initial letters of all the words in that sentence to make up new words in as many other 'satisfactory sentences' as they can. For example, if you write the sentence *Mary had a little lamb*, individuals or groups of children should attempt to make up as many sentences as they can in which the words start with the letters *M*, *h*, *a*, *l*, and *l*, no matter how ridiculous. For example: *My hat always looks lovely*.

■ A different version of the game can be played based around the number seven. Ask the children to write a short story comprising seven 'satisfactory sentences'. Each sentence must have only seven words. The same game can be played with other numbers so that children of different abilities can play.

TONGUE-TWISTER GYMNASTICS

OBJECTIVES

To enable children to:
■ practise oral language skills, especially careful listening and enunciation
■ reinforce understanding of the single complete sentence
■ consolidate understanding of alliteration.

RESOURCES AND CLASSROOM ORGANIZATION

Before introducing this activity to the class, you should prepare a small collection of five or six single-sentence tongue-twisters on the board or flip chart. You will also need a clock with a second hand, or a minute timer.

This game can be played by any number of children from two to the whole class.

WHAT TO DO

Begin by asking the children if they know what tongue-twisters are and if they can say any. If the children are unsure, explain that a tongue-twister is a sentence or phrase that is made up of words that either begin with the same letter or have the same sounds and that are very difficult to say quickly and correctly.

You could begin with the old favourite *Peter Piper picked a peck of pickled pepper. How many pecks of pickled pepper did Peter Piper pick?* and then try *Round the rugged rocks the ragged rascals ran* and *Three thoughtful thrushes flew through the thicket.*

To start 'Tongue-twister gymnastics', which is a very simple game, appoint one child as a timekeeper and another as the first player. The class or group should then decide upon a tongue-twister from your prepared collection. The player is allowed to say the chosen sentence slowly twice just to get their tongue into training! Then the timekeeper shouts *Go!* and the player has to say the tongue-twister as many times as possible in one minute. The rest of the class or group must keep count of how many times the sentence is said correctly. After one minute the timekeeper calls out *Stop!* and the listeners declare the score, that is to say, the number of times the player said the tongue-twister correctly in the minute. A new challenger for the tongue-twisting gymnastics should then be asked to step forward.

DIFFERENTIATION

Ask the children to work in groups to write sentences where most of the words contain the same sound. For example: *Jack carried his black backpack along the track to his shack.* These sentences will often turn into tongue-twisters which children will enjoy reading at speed to each other.

NOW OR LATER

Groups of children could go on a tongue-twister hunt in the library, searching through poetry and rhyme collections to find sentences that only use words beginning with the same letter. You could then build up a class collection of tongue-twisters. You could also organize a short ceremony to crown the child who can recite these alliterative sentences most fluently as King or Queen of 'Tongue-twister gymnastics'.

Use the following tongue-twister sentences to start your collection:

> Some sunshine shone on Simon's shiny shoes.
> The sixth sheik's sixth sheep's sick.
> What noise annoys a noisy oyster? A noisy noise annoys a noisy oyster.
> An ancient Armenian angered an armadillo.

PLAUSIBLE PROVERBS

RESOURCES AND CLASSROOM ORGANIZATION

You will need to prepare a selection of well-known and less well-known proverbs to use as a resource before introducing this activity. Some examples from this selection could be written on the board or flip chart. You will need a copy of photocopiable page 50 for each child, writing materials, paper and a Bible (optional).

Children work as a whole class, then individually or in groups.

WHAT TO DO

Talk to the children about the title of the game and ensure that they understand what proverbs are and how they are used. Explain that they are short, wise sayings about an experience or fact that usually offer advice or guidance. Alternatively, you could just introduce the word 'proverb' and briefly explain what it means. The children could then work in groups and research some examples of proverbs in the school library.

You could then go on to discuss some of the proverbs on the board or some that the children have discovered in their research. You could also mention that there is a book called 'Proverbs' in the Bible and read out some examples to the class. A further discussion about the language used in the proverbs from different sources could then ensue.

Once the sayings are understood, give out a copy of photocopiable page 50 to each child to work on individually or in groups. In the first part of the activity the children are asked to match the beginning of each proverb with its correct ending.

OBJECTIVES

To enable children to:
- understand and become familiar with proverbs
- learn to manipulate language by turning old proverbs into new versions.

On the second part of the photocopiable sheet, the children are asked to complete some well-known proverbs with alternative endings of their own. For example:

> Half a loaf… leaves you hungry.
> Where there's a will… there's a dead person.
> People in glass houses… should always wear clothes.
> Still water… usually smells.

Much delight and laughter can be enjoyed from these inventions, which should be shared amongst the class at the end of the activity.

Answers to photocopiable page 50
Don't count your chickens before they are hatched.
You can't make an omelette without breaking eggs.
When in Rome, do as the Romans do.
Don't cross your bridges before you come to them.
Don't cry over spilt milk.
A bird in the hand is worth two in the bush.
Where there's a will there's a way.
Still waters run deep.
Half a loaf is better than none.
People in glass houses shouldn't throw stones.
Always look before you leap.
Empty vessels make the most noise.

DIFFERENTIATION

Less able children may need adult support to complete the activity on the photocopiable sheet. These children may enjoy illustrating some of the 'plausible proverbs' from the photocopiable sheet or some of the other sayings that have been discussed in class. This work could then be displayed around the classroom or included in a class book of proverbs.

Children who have no difficulty with the activity on the photocopiable sheet may enjoy inventing their own 'plausible proverbs' from scratch. These could be nonsensical, cynical or serious, for example: *You can't walk far in a shoe with no sole.*

Some of these invented proverbs may fall flat, but others will seem entirely plausible. Discuss some of the children's ideas, and the best ones could be included in a class book.

NOW OR LATER

■ Ask the children to collect some proverbs from their parents or grandparents and discuss some of the more unusual or obscure examples in class. Any new proverbs they bring could be added to the class book and illustrated or displayed in the classroom.

■ The children could try to translate some proverbs into their own words, making sure that their translation explains the meaning of the original.

IMPROVING SENTENCES

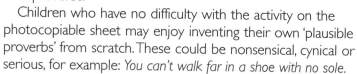

OBJECTIVES
To enable children to:
■ extend their vocabulary
■ think carefully about word choices
■ consolidate their knowledge of verbs and synonyms.

RESOURCES AND CLASSROOM ORGANIZATION
You will need a board or flip chart, writing materials and paper.
Children work as a whole class and then in pairs.

WHAT TO DO
Ask the children to talk about their weekend activities and write some of these down as sentences on the board or flip chart. Discuss some of the sentences with

the class, placing particular emphasis upon the verbs contained in each one. Then ask individual children to come up and underline a verb in one of the sentences until they are all underlined.

Choose one verb and demonstrate how, by substituting a stronger, more specific verb, the meaning of the sentence can be sharpened and strengthened. Explain that a synonym is a word similar in meaning to another word; it is a word that in most contexts can be substituted for another without affecting the meaning. For example: *ship/vessel*, *monster/beast* or *laughed/giggled*.

Now ask the children to write a sentence of their own at the top of their paper and hand it to a partner. The partner must find a synonym, or synonyms, for any of the words in the sentence and write these words underneath. The idea is to improve or strengthen the original sentence. For example, if the original sentence is: *I walked home feeling very tired*, the improving sentence might be: *I shuffled home feeling very weary*.

DIFFERENTIATION

You could introduce a competitive element into this activity by writing a simple, or more complex, sentence on the board, depending on the abilities of the children, and then asking individuals, pairs or small groups to invent as many different versions as they can, changing one word each time. They should only use synonyms and avoid changing the meaning of the sentence. For example:

> The animal ran towards them making a terrible noise.
> The animal ran towards them making a terrible *sound*.
> The *beast* ran towards them making a terrible sound.
> The beast *charged* towards them making a terrible sound.
> The beast charged towards them making a *horrible* sound.

And so on.

Before they attempt this activity, less able children might be given a list of words and asked to write two words that are the same or similar in meaning to these words.

NOW OR LATER

■ The revised sentences could be examined in a general class discussion at the end of the session and decisions made about which sentences now have stronger language.

■ You could create an ongoing class thesaurus by writing particular words across the top of a large sheet of paper and asking the children to write synonyms on self-adhesive labels or Post-it Notes to be placed underneath.

NEW SIMILES

RESOURCES AND CLASSROOM ORGANIZATION

A small amount of preparation is needed for this activity. You should collect a selection of similes from a variety of written sources as well as inventing some of your own. You will also need a copy of photocopiable page 51 for each child, writing materials and paper.

Children can work in small groups or pairs, or together as a whole class.

OBJECTIVES

To enable children to:
■ understand the nature of a simile
■ practise using imaginative language.

45

WHAT TO DO

Before starting this activity explain the nature of a simile – that it is a comparison for effect or illustration. Read some examples to the class that you have found in poems, some that are well known, or some that you have invented. For example:

> The snow looked like cotton wool.
> Snow White had cheeks like ripe cherries.
> I wander'd lonely as a cloud.

Ask the children if they know any similes and discuss the language used in them and the images they connote. Each child should now complete photocopiable page 51.

In the first part of this activity the children are given a list of words and they use these words to write sentences that create evocative images using the format of a simile in each one. For example: Hungry: *I feel as hungry as an elephant with a knot tied in its trunk.*

For the second part of the photocopiable sheet, the children are given some sentence beginnings and they choose from a list the best second part that contains an appropriate and imaginative simile.

DIFFERENTIATION

More able children should be encouraged to use their imagination to find the most unusual simile they can. You might explain and experiment with anthropomorphic imagery by asking the children to connect objects with imagery to do with different creatures. For example:

> The trees… were like huge stalking giants
> Her tongue… flicked out like that of a venomous snake.

NOW OR LATER

Ask the children to work in pairs or small groups and make a list of possible endings to go with the start of the image. For example:

> He had a voice…
>   like snapping twigs
>   like ripe plums
>   like a referee's whistle
>   like a croaking frog
>
> Other simile starters might be:
>
>   The tom cat's purr…
>   The old oak tree…
>   She had hair…
>   The singer's trousers…
>   His front door bell…
>   The footballer's tattoo…

Award a prize for the most imaginative simile, or to the group that has invented the most similes for each sentence starter.

NAME SENTENCES

OBJECTIVES

To enable children to
■ learn to manipulate language
■ consolidate understanding of the single complete sentence.

RESOURCES AND CLASSROOM ORGANIZATION

You will need writing materials and paper.

This game can be played in pairs or groups. It is deceptively easy but does require supervision.

WHAT TO DO

Divide the children into pairs or groups and choose a child to spell out the letters of their name. The other children now have to write a sentence in which the first letter of each word matches the letters of the name in the correct order. For example, if the name called out is *John*, a sentence might be: *Jim opened his notebook.* If the name shouted out is *Christine* or *William*, however, the task becomes far more difficult but not impossible. For the name *William* a sentence might be: *Why is little Lesley in a mood?*

This game is far more difficult than it might at first appear, so nonsense sentences should be allowed so long as they are grammatically correct.

The game may be played collaboratively or competitively. If played competitively then the first individual or pair to make a correct sentence scores a point. It is possibly better played as a collaborative effort to see what interesting sentences can be made.

DIFFERENTIATION

For more able children you could score the game by counting word syllables. The players must not only make a correct sentence using the letters of a name, but also consider using the longest words possible in order to score highly in each round.

Less able children might concentrate on writing sentences for shorter names of three of four letters.

NOW OR LATER

■ Ask each group to give a name to another group who must then attempt to write as many different sentences as they can using the letters of that name. The group who can invent the most sentences is the winner. For example, if the name is *Harry* then the sentences might be: *Happy Anna ran races yesterday. Has another relative repaid you?*

■ Acrostic poems: Explain to the children that poets often use visual tricks to help to organize their poems. Help the children to choose a topic and a key word that sums up that topic. Write the key word vertically down the page. Then for each letter think of a word or phrase, starting with that letter, that has some connection with the topic. For example, a child might write:

> **S**hrieking
> **C**hildren laughing
> **H**appy faces
> **O**bedience forgotten
> **O**rder gone
> **L**ine up now

Words that describe the weather, the names of the seasons or the months of the year could be used as key words.

You could start a class collection of acrostic poems.

O'GRADY SAYS

RESOURCES AND CLASSROOM ORGANIZATION

To play this game you will need to make a pack of 20 or so instruction cards, large enough for the children to read at a distance. These cards should contain a set of instructions of increasing complexity. The first few cards could contain simple ones, such as: *Stand up, turn around and sit down* or: *Stand up, put your hands in the air and sit down*. However, some of the cards should introduce a more complex set of actions. For example: *Stand up, then hold up your book, read one sentence, close the book, sit down and cross your arms*. The instructions should be varied and some of them should generate amusement, such as: *Stand on one leg and sing one line of a song*.

The game can be played by large groups or by the whole class. Supervision is required.

WHAT TO DO

Some children may already be familiar with the oral version of the game 'O'Grady says'. This is a written version and is simple to play.

Divide the children into two teams. Hold up a card, wait until several children have read the card and have their hand up, and then nominate someone to perform the actions required. If the player does this correctly they score a point for their team. If they perform the actions or instructions in the wrong order, or forget an instruction, a player from another team takes a turn.

The cards should be briskly presented and then put away, so the players must concentrate upon what they are reading in order to remember what to do.

DIFFERENTIATION

The instructions on the question cards can vary in difficulty so that children of all abilities can play the game. You could prepare a set of question cards for particularly fluent readers to respond to. These cards, which can be quickly made, might include such questions as *What is the time? Where is my pen? What is the name of the headteacher?* These are then flashed at the group, for a few seconds or less, with the first child to answer correctly scoring a point.

NOW OR LATER

■ Some groups could write their own sentence cards and play the game without supervision. The group should sit in a semicircle with one player standing in the centre showing the card to the other members of the group one at a time. If the player to whom the card is shown performs the actions required on the card correctly, they replace the player in the centre.

■ 'Living sentences' is another simple game using flash cards. In this game the children each have single word cards and run out to the front of the class to form sentences given by you. The rest of the class then confirms whether or not the line they form makes the correct word order for the sentence.

■ As another variation you could play 'Sentence completion'. In this game each child in a pair writes a sentence on a slip of paper, and leaves out one word, which should be fairly easy to guess from the context. Each slip is then passed to the next child, who fills in the missing word. They then write another incomplete sentence on the paper and pass it back to the first child. The first child corrects the attempt at completion, if necessary, completes the second sentence and adds an incomplete third to pass back to their partner, and so on.

CLOZE RACES

OBJECTIVE
To enable children to:
■ practise careful reading
■ practise the use of context cues.

RESOURCES AND CLASSROOM ORGANIZATION

For this activity you will need to prepare lists of about ten sentences (depending upon the size of the teams) with a word or words missing (marked by a line or row of dots) and write these on large sheets of paper. Place them on a row of desks at the front of the classroom. The lists should be identical, but the sentences should be in a different order on different sheets. The missing word or words ought to be such that they can be guessed from context. For example:

> The train standing at ___ seven is ready to leave.
> Once upon a ___ a witch flew on her ___ over the forest.
> London is England's capital ___.
> As soon ___ he saw her he knew she was special.

This is a whole-class activity in which the children work in teams. Some supervision is required.

WHAT TO DO

Cloze exercises are well-known activities for encouraging children to interrogate a text by using context cues to guess the meaning of missing words. This game simplifies the procedure and turns it into a competition.

Arrange the children into teams, each team being allocated one desk with a list of sentences to complete. One member of each team then runs out to the front of the classroom, reads the first sentence, writes in the missing word or words, then runs back to their place. The second member of the team then runs out, reads the second sentence, and writes the missing word or words in the second sentence. The third player does the same, and so on.

Make sure the children understand that if the second player writes an incorrect word you will cross it out and the third team member must try to correct it before the team can move on to the third sentence. The first team to complete all the sentences on their paper correctly wins the game.

DIFFERENTIATION

Instead of separate sentences, a continuous passage can be used, with players filling in one gap at a time when they run up for their turn. The complexity of the sentences should vary for more and less able children.

In this version delete every fifth or seventh word, ensuring that the context cues allow the gap to be filled. Players will often have to read large sections of the passage in order to fill in 'their' gap. You should be lenient in allowing alternatives to the original deletions so long as these answers are syntactically and grammatically correct.

NOW OR LATER

You could play the game to consolidate players' understanding of a particular aspect of language. There are a variety of ways to create a cloze passage. For example:
■ delete particular pieces of 'technical' vocabulary in a non-fiction passage
■ delete particular parts of speech, perhaps verbs, pronouns or conjunctions
■ delete punctuation, putting a line where each item of punctuation should be.

Plausible proverbs

■ These proverbs have the wrong endings. Match the beginning of each proverb to its correct ending.

Don't count your chickens	over spilt milk.
You can't make an omelette	before you come to them.
When in Rome,	there's a way.
Don't cross your bridges	before they are hatched.
Don't cry	before you leap.
A bird in the hand	shouldn't throw stones.
Where there's a will	do as the Romans do.
Still waters	make the most noise.
Half a loaf is	worth two in the bush.
People in glass houses	run deep.
Always look	without breaking eggs.
Empty vessels	is better than none.

■ Write some new endings to these proverbs. Try and make them as unusual and funny as possible. The first one has been done for you.

A bird in the hand *can make a nasty mess.*

Half a loaf _____

Where there's a will _____

People in glass houses _____

Still waters _____

Always look before you _____

Ready to go! WORD GAMES FOR LITERACY

New similes

■ Write a sentence about each of the words below using similes to create an unusual or amusing image. For example:

Hungry
I feel as hungry as an elephant with a knot tied in its trunk.

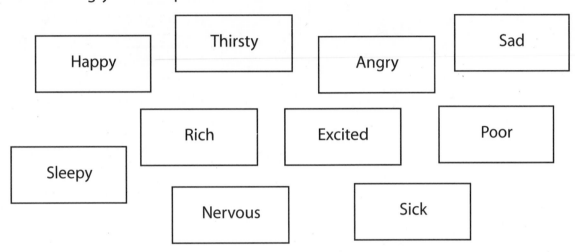

Happy	Thirsty	Angry	Sad

Rich   Excited   Poor

Sleepy

Nervous   Sick

■ Below are some sentence beginnings. From the list at the bottom of the page, choose the best and most imaginative simile to complete each sentence.

The frozen leaves crunched underfoot like

Old Albert's sneeze was like

The enormous crocodile laughed so much his teeth rattled like

In the freezing weather the birds were puffed up like

The window shutters were bulging as if

The river ran through the valley like

The Catherine Wheels spun round like

crisp, dry cornflakes.

a long silver snake.

whirling, swirling marigolds.

a huge cannon going off.

coins in a moneybox.

woolly balls.

tired elephants were leaning against them.

 **Section 4**   **GAMES WITH TEXTS**

This section gives children the chance to play games using whole texts or large segments of texts. There are games, for instance, to help children learn techniques that writers employ to convey what they want to say succinctly or dramatically or in rhyme. All the games are designed to help children towards satisfaction with the way they use language.

The games in this section focus particularly on:
- introducing different text types, such as biography
- introducing different poetic forms, such as haiku, and cinquain
- teaching punctuation and sentence construction
- giving practice with skim-reading and locating information
- giving practice in story-building skills, for example sequencing narrative and writing dialogue
- developing comprehension skills.

COMPREHENSION PUZZLES

OBJECTIVE
To enable children to:
develop comprehension and
logical thinking skills.

RESOURCES AND CLASSROOM ORGANIZATION

Before introducing this activity you need to prepare some short stories, each with a single inference for the children to work out. You will need writing materials and paper.

WHAT TO DO

Simply read out your examples for the children to answer. The answers could be read aloud and the children asked to explain how they decided on them, or small groups could discuss their responses together. The stories used might be very simple, or they might be slightly more difficult (like the third and fourth examples here):

> The teacher gave everyone in class a note to take home. The note told parents about an event for the class the next day that would involve a coach trip. Everyone had to come to school at eight o'clock, one hour before school normally starts. When Tim arrived at school the next morning at the usual time there was no one there. *Where were they?*
>
> Mrs Wood had just put some cakes in the oven when the phone rang. When her son William arrived home from school his mother was still on the phone and there was a funny smell in the house. *What was the smell?*
>
> Mr Brown put on his coat and gloves to go out into the garden. He started digging the wet ground. After a while he went indoors for a cup of hot soup. *What season might it be?*
>
> I am lying back in a chair. There is a big light above my head and a man in a white coat next to me. *Where am I?*

DIFFERENTIATION

More able children could write their own comprehension puzzles. These should be short stories with a question at the end, and there should be enough clues to infer the answer. These could be shared with the class at the end of the session.

NOW OR LATER

■ You could play a different version of comprehension puzzles with stories that have a slightly disguised, internal inconsistency, where the question at the end is always *What is wrong?* For example:

> Dan woke at dawn ready for the lion hunt. He wanted to photograph the biggest pride of lions in Africa. It wasn't long before he picked up the trail of lion footprints in the soft earth. Just as the heat of the day made him sit down for a drink, there, right in front of him, appeared a huge male lion, its teeth bared, and its eyes glinting in the moonlight. *What is wrong?*

Ask the class in groups to write a collection of stories like these and arrange to present them for the rest of the class to solve.

■ You could play a very simple game that also requires the children to listen intently and think carefully. You will need to provide a list of a set of words and a question that asks the children to identify just one word in the list. The children should answer orally. For example, if the question is: *Which word includes the meaning of all the others?* the list might be: *banana, fruit, apple, orange, plum* or *Belgium, Norway, country, Spain, Australia* or *swallow, wren, thrush, bird, cuckoo.* If the question is: *Which word means something larger than the others?* then the list might be: *goldfish, shark, trout, salmon, stickleback* or *decade, year, century, month, week* or *cottage, flat, bungalow, mansion, mews.*

TWO TRUTHS AND A LIE

RESOURCES AND CLASSROOM ORGANIZATION

This activity requires a brief introduction to explain the differences between biography and autobiography. Examples of each type of text might be useful to show to the class. You will need writing materials and paper.

The children could work either in groups or as a whole class.

WHAT TO DO

Introduce this activity by explaining to the class what biography and autobiography are and the differences between them. You could also remind the children at this point about the differences between fiction and non-fiction texts. Then ask the children to write a one-paragraph excerpt from their autobiography. Their excerpt must contain two accurate facts and one piece of total fiction about themselves.

If the children are working in a group they should sit in a circle. Choose one child to be the guesser, who should stand in the centre. The game begins when the guesser points to someone in the circle and asks them to read out their autobiographical paragraph. The guesser must then decide which statement in the paragraph is false. If the guesser is correct they change places with the writer, who becomes the new guesser. If the guess is incorrect, the writer must not reveal which statement is fiction, and the guesser must try again with another writer. Play continues until everyone in the circle has had a chance to read out their two truths and one lie.

DIFFERENTIATION

More able children could play a different version of this game using biographical, rather than autobiographical statements. They could research and then write two

OBJECTIVE

To enable children to: become familiar with autobiography text and the notion of biographical facts.

53

truths and one lie about a famous person, alive or dead. Alternatively, they could write (two truths and a lie) about a fictional character, for example, Harry Potter or Sherlock Holmes, and then play the game using these paragraphs. A discussion could follow the playing of these games about the relationship of fiction and non-fiction and biography.

Less able children could be given a list of appropriate words and phrases to help them to write their autobiographical paragraph and suggestions of well-known people about whom they could write two truths and a lie.

NOW OR LATER

Once the standard version of the game has been played, it can be repeated in reverse (two lies and one truth). This time the children could write a paragraph of fiction about themselves, but include one sentence of truth which has to be guessed by the other players.

CUT-UP POETRY

OBJECTIVES

To enable children to:
■ think carefully about language, word by word
■ appreciate the nature of poetic form.

RESOURCES AND CLASSROOM ORGANIZATION

For this activity you will need a fairly large selection of newspapers and magazines for the children to cut up, small paper bags, scissors, glue and plain paper. It may also be useful to have some dictionaries available for inquiring minds to find out what some of their words mean.

Before introducing the activity you could try it out for yourself and show the children your cut-up poem as an example, before they start work.

The children can work individually, in pairs or small groups.

WHAT TO DO

This activity may at first appear to be anarchy but it can in fact produce a broad range of different styles of poem.

Each child should take one or more pages from the supply of newspapers and magazines. They should then carefully cut out individual words that take their fancy. Their selection should include small words such as *to*, and, *in*, as well as longer words such as *frightening*, *solitude*, *celebrate* or *memorial*. Each child should then put his or her chosen words into a paper bag. When they have a reasonable number, ask them to shake the bag and pull out one word at a time. As the words are pulled out the children should try to organize them into whatever poetic shape seems suitable. When they are happy with the result, tell them to glue the words into place on the plain paper as their cut-up poem.

DIFFERENTIATION

More able children could cut out and work with phrases rather than individual words, and include adjectival and noun phrases as well as longer five- or six-word phrases. Suggest that when they are putting their cut-up poem together they might want to return to the magazine or newspaper to look for another word that might help to make the poem work better.

NOW OR LATER

■ Children could read their cut-up poems to one another or to the whole class at the end of the session.
■ Display the cut-up poems around the classroom.
■ Encourage the children to talk about how they organized their random collection of words and why they chose the order and line format that they have.

QUATRAINS AND CINQUAINS

RESOURCES AND CLASSROOM ORGANIZATION
You should give an introduction to the class about rhyming patterns as they relate to quatrains and cinquains. You will need writing materials and paper and copies of photocopiable page 62 (for 'Now or later' activity).

The children work in groups of four.

WHAT TO DO
Explain the possible patterns for rhyme in a four-line verse – ABAB or AABB or ABBA. The first player in a group gives a word and the second player then has to give a word that rhymes with that first word. The third player gives a word, and the fourth player must offer a word that rhymes with the third word. For example, one child could say *white*, and another say *fight*. A third child could say *spit* and finally a fourth say *hit*. Now the group must invent a quatrain using the given words, in any rhyming order, at the end of the lines. For example, for an ABAB pattern:

When Peter got hit
He turned quite white
So he started to spit
And got in a fight

For an AABB pattern, the verse could read:

When Peter got hit
He started to spit
Ann turned quite white
When she saw the fight

And for an ABBA pattern:

Peter got in a fight
And started to spit
But when he got hit
His face turned quite white

The groups can be asked to produce one quatrain, or three versions using the different patterns but the same rhyming words. After a suitable period for invention, groups are asked to read out their rhymes to each other. They might then swap the quatrains and be asked to improve on, or offer alternative versions of, the originals.

DIFFERENTIATION
Children with good language skills will be able to invent quatrains independently. Each member of a group of five is given pairs of rhyming words to work with by the other four members, and then has to invent a quatrain on their own using those words. They should be allowed the help of a dictionary and thesaurus if they wish.

NOW OR LATER
■ Groups might go on a quatrain hunt in the library, searching through poetry and rhyme collections to find quatrains with different rhyme patterns. Build up a class collection of quatrains.
■ Organize a class vote on the top ten quatrains discovered or invented.
■ Repeat the activities outlined above with other simple non-rhyming poetic forms, using photocopiable page 62 to remind them of syllable patterns, for example with Haiku: 3 lines of 5, 7, and then 5 syllables; Tanka: 5 lines of 31 syllables used in the following way: 5, 7, 5, 7, 7.

Objectives
To enable children to:
■ understand the possible rhyming patterns in a four-line stanza
■ practice syllabification skills with a five-line stanza.

Cinquains are 5-line, blank-verse shape poems. They normally have 22 syllables in the pattern 2, 4, 6, 8, 2. Although it is not necessary to follow this pattern, counting the number of syllables they use in each line is good for encouraging syllabification skills. So a child might end up with something like this:

> Snow falls
> Falling slowly
> Falling falling slowly
> Falling falling slowly, slowly
> Snow falls

It is of course possible to experiment with non-standard cinquains. A cinquain writer might concentrate upon words rather than syllables. For instance, ask children to produce a five-line stanza adding one word more per line. So:

> Snow
> Snow falls
> Snow falls slowly
> Snow falls slowly drifting
> Snow falls slowly drifting down

Or try writing a cinquain where every line contains more letters than the last. So:

> I
> Love
> White
> Snowflakes
> Slowly falling

DRAMATIC PUNCTUATION

OBJECTIVES

To enable children to:
- practise reading skills
- gain an understanding of punctuation and sentence construction.

RESOURCES AND CLASSROOM ORGANIZATION

Before this lesson you will need to find a short piece of prose (preferably fiction) that is rich in punctuation marks: full stops, commas, questions marks, speech marks and capital letters. You will also need a board or flip chart or an OHP. Write your selected piece on the board or OHT before the session.

The game can be played by large groups or by the whole class together. Be warned: this can be a very noisy activity and instruction and supervision will be required throughout!

WHAT TO DO

The purpose of this game is to turn all the punctuation in a piece of prose into both speech and action. Write some different punctuation marks on the board and before starting the game spend some time with the whole class discussing the different punctuation marks and what they do in a sentence. Then decide upon a sound effect for each one. For example: the children may like to clap for a full stop, click their fingers for a comma, say *mmm* for a question mark, pop fingers against the inside of their cheeks for speech marks, and so on. Record their suggestions on the board.

Then show the children your chosen text and display it so that the whole group or class can read it, making audible the various punctuation marks as discussed. Once this has been mastered the group must decide upon a suitable action to go with each sound. For example: if a capital letter is marked by the sound *zing*, then it may be decided that at the same time the children must beat their chests; or if a full stop is marked by a *sss* sound, the group may agree that the action to go with this is a deep bow. The class can experiment to find suitable actions that can be performed (without injury!), such as throwing hands in the air, pirouetting or stamping. Their choices for actions should be noted on the board, next to the sounds, to become their 'script'.

The performance can cause much hilarity, even a cacophony. The 'script' must be visible to the whole class. It is best if someone is chosen to be the conductor for this 'symphony'. The conductor should point to the text as it is read and the rest of the 'orchestra' performs the punctuation on cue.

DIFFERENTIATION

More able children may wish to write their own dramatic punctuation stories once they have understood how the game works. Their stories could then be performed in small groups to the rest of the class. Do not be surprised if you hear similar noises when the children are supposed to be writing quietly!

NOW OR LATER

■ You could arrange for the class to perform the game at an assembly to the rest of the school. Or, alternatively, organize a performance at a school concert for parents, who should be asked to join in by performing the actions and sound effects themselves.

■ A similar game can be played with spelling, instead of punctuation. Draw up a list of words that the players should be able to spell. Then choose someone to be the quizmaster. The quizmaster must then tell the players the two letters that no one is allowed to say. For example, it might be the letters t and e. Instead of saying the forbidden letters the players must perform an action – for example, a salute for t and a head scratch for e. The quizmaster should then ask each player in turn to spell a word from the agreed list. They must then perform the action instead of speaking the forbidden letters. It is fun to ban letters that occur often in words. Banning the letter s makes words such as *mistress*, *dismissive* and *Mississippi* quite difficult to spell!

TREASURE HUNT

RESOURCES AND CLASSROOM ORGANIZATION

Before playing this game you will need to collect a variety of newspapers and cut out several stories from them that are suitable for the children to read. You should then give one story to each pair or group as well as a copy of one of the treasure hunt score cards on photocopiable page 63. The object of the game is to go 'hunting for treasure' in the stories. The 'treasure' takes the form of punctuation marks or prefixes and suffixes. Before play begins you must decide how much each treasure item is worth but keep this information secret until later in the game. For instance, you might value full stops at just £1, but question marks at £4.

You will need copies of newspaper stories, photocopiable page 63, writing materials, highlighter pens (optional) and paper.

This is a game that focuses upon locating information and can be adapted to a range of purposes.

Any number of children can play from two to the whole class, although the activity is probably best done in pairs or small groups.

WHAT TO DO

Before play begins, discuss different punctuation marks with the children and ensure that they understand the terms 'prefix' and 'suffix'. Explain that the object of the game is to go searching through the newspaper stories for 'treasure'.

OBJECTIVES
To enable the children to:
■ develop familiarity with punctuation, prefixes and suffixes
■ practise skim-reading.

57

Ready to go! WORD GAMES FOR LITERACY

Set a time limit for the game and advise the players that they should skim through the text looking for items of punctuation, prefixes and suffixes. Each time they find one they should draw a circle around it, or use a highlighter pen and put a tally mark on the score card on the photocopiable sheet in the appropriate column.

When time is up, or when players have finished checking the whole of their story (whichever comes first), they should add up the number of treasure items in each column. At this point you should announce how much each piece of treasure is worth. Each player should then work out the total value of his or her tally sheet. The player with the most valuable total find is the winner of that round.

DIFFERENTIATION

This is a game that can be adapted for a number of purposes, and to the ability of the pupils. Score cards might be made for particular parts of speech. For example, you could organize a treasure hunt for pronouns, or proper nouns, or for conjunctions. You can also vary the length and complexity of the newspaper articles in order to accommodate groups of more or less able children.

NOW OR LATER

Use the same game format to 'hunt' for:
■ spelling patterns such as final e, or ie; double letters; -tion endings
■ particular phonemes, such as the digraphs sh, th, ph and ch
■ at least ten adjectives
■ at least ten words beginning with the letter p
■ words of more than three syllables.

THE WRITING FRAME GAME

OBJECTIVES

To enable children to:
■ develop an understanding of sequencing in writing
■ develop story-building skills and creative confidence.

RESOURCES AND CLASSROOM ORGANIZATION

Before this lesson, you should make writing frames, one per child, which provide sentence starts and writing frames for stories (see 'What to do'). You will also need long sheets of paper and writing materials.

The children work in groups of three or four, each sitting in a circle at a table.

WHAT TO DO

Introduce this activity by talking to the children about stories and opening sentences. These are usually of vital importance as they have to capture the reader's interest and imagination and make them want to read on to find out what happens next.

Explain to the children that they are going to write a story together as a group with each member writing a sentence in turn. However, they are not going to know what their story is really about until they have finished it!

One child in each group should write, using the writing frame, the opening words of their story on the top of the long sheet of paper. For example, if you have provided the opening *Once upon a time…* the writer copies this and completes this opening sentence. They then fold the paper over to cover the words and pass it on to the next child who copies their sentence start from the next part of the writing frame and completes the sentence. The third player does the same, and so on.

The paper can go around the table more than once until each sentence start has been used. The paper is then unfolded to reveal the, no doubt surreal, story. At the end of the session, one member from each group could be chosen to read out their story to be enjoyed by the whole class.

Sentence starts for the writing frame could include:

> But…
> Still…
> Then along came…
> Nevertheless…
> Turning the corner…
> While…
> When…
> And yet…
> Afterwards…
> However…
> Meanwhile…
> So…

DIFFERENTIATION

There are many possible variations to this game. The writing frame supplied by the teacher might give more or less direction depending on the ability of the children. As an alternative to the above version the children could be asked to write their own conjoining phrases or words, or they could start the game by constructing their own writing frame themselves. Or you could provide the opening words and some sentence starts, which could be quite specific. For example:

> It was midnight and the wind howled across the deserted village.
> Then…
> After a while…
> But nobody knew their secret, which was…
> So they…
> After that…

NOW OR LATER

Considering variations for this game is a creative challenge in itself. The children could, for example, use the game format but agree to keep the content within a certain genre, perhaps to create a crazy fairy story, or a science fiction tale, or a ghost story. The teacher might use the game to draw attention to the way sentences can be joined together, or as a starting point for considering how effectively sequences in stories follow on.

FABULOUS FICTION

RESOURCES AND CLASSROOM ORGANIZATION

Some preparation time is required on the first occasion this game is played. A few days before you introduce the game to the class, ask the children to bring in any unwanted magazines, brochures, shopping catalogues, advertisement flyers and other 'junk mail' publications that have small photos or illustrations in them. The pictures need to be small enough to fit onto index cards, so you will need to check that the material brought into class is appropriate. You will also need several sets of index cards, scissors and glue.

The game is played in groups of up to eight.

OBJECTIVE

To enable children to: develop story building skills and creative confidence.

WHAT TO DO

Explain to the children that for the first part of this game they are going on a 'picture hunt'. Give each pair or group a number of different publications and ask them to

look through them for photographs of single objects or people, or simple images. When they find some they should cut them out carefully. Remind the children that the pictures have to be small enough to fit onto the index cards.

Once a collection of pictures has been gathered, check the selection to ensure there is plenty of variety. Give out the index cards and ask the children to paste the pictures onto the cards. The children should have at least five cards each. If you intend to continue to use the same cards you may wish to laminate them.

The players should now sit around tables in groups, or in circles on the floor. One player should be chosen as the 'dealer'. The dealer should shuffle the index cards and deal five to each player. The players must leave the cards face down. The first player now turns over their first card and begins a story containing a reference to whatever the picture is on the upturned card. For example, if the card shows a picture of a train:

> Tom Turrell, the famous detective, had been on many train journeys in his life, but he felt somehow that this one was going to be special. He boarded the European Express at eight o'clock and it left promptly at ten minutes past…

Now the second player turns up their top card. It could be a picture of a man in dark glasses. The story does not have to be serious, or even believable. The fiction can be as fabulous as the players want to make it. So the second player may decide to take the story in a different direction:

> No sooner had the train left the station than a man in dark glasses sat down next to Tom. Very soon the strangest thing happened. The man in dark glasses appeared to be gradually shrinking…

After this, the third player turns over a card which shows a picture of… a microwave oven! This player has somehow to use their ingenuity to continue the story, making reference to the picture on the card. The game continues, normally with much amusement, with the players each turning a card over in turn until all the cards have been used.

DIFFERENTIATION

A written version of this activity might be played with confident writers. The cards should be shuffled and five cards dealt to each player and placed in the middle of the group, this time face up. Players must write their made-up stories using the five images on the table in front of them.

This game can be made more or less difficult depending on whether it is a rule that the images must be used in a certain order. You could also increase or decrease the number of pictures that the players have to use depending on their ability. When the children have finished, the players should take turns to read their stories aloud to each other. A class discussion could follow about their different story solutions to the five pictures.

NOW OR LATER

Play the game as a team activity. Place five enlarged pictures on display where the whole class can see them. The children should play in small groups and work together to write a short 'fabulous fiction'. One member of each group should be chosen to be the scribe. A time limit could be placed on the writing time, and then one member from each team should read out their story. Alternatively, the teams might be asked to create the fiction against the clock, with the first team to complete their story being designated winners and asked to read out their 'fabulous fiction' to the rest. As before, you may wish to increase or decrease the number of pictures displayed to match the age and abilities of the players.

CRAZY CARTOONS

OBJECTIVE

To enable children to:
learn how to write a short,
coherent story using dialogue
only.

RESOURCES AND CLASSROOM ORGANIZATION

Before introducing this activity you will need to make a collection of newspapers and children's comics and magazines that contain cartoon strips. You will also need scissors, correcting fluid or 'white-out' pens and felt-tipped pens.

This activity is best completed in pairs.

WHAT TO DO

Introduce the activity by talking to the children about some of the cartoons that they enjoy in magazines or comics. Ask them what they have noticed about the language used in the pictures. The children may have some favourite cartoon characters who have stock words or phrases that they can repeat.

Divide the children into pairs and ask them to cut out two or three short cartoon strips from the newspapers or comics you have collected. The pairs should then work together and carefully 'white out' the words inside the speech bubbles and write in some text or dialogue that gives meaning to the set of pictures. At the end of the session the cartoon strips can be exchanged so that the children read each other's work.

It is sometimes difficult to write over correcting fluid – so you may wish to white out some of the speech bubbles yourself. It is also not good to expose children to correcting fluid for too long as it is toxic. You could then make enlarged photocopies of the cartoon strips and give the altered copies to the pairs who then have to write in their own new dialogue using the picture clues. The children can compare their different versions when all the cartoons are complete. There could be a class vote on the best cartoon story.

DIFFERENTIATION

Ask the more able artists in the class to draw a six-frame cartoon story, leaving space for speech bubbles in each frame. They can then pass this strip to a friend who is not so good at drawing to write in the speech to make a complete cartoon.

NOW OR LATER

As an additional activity you could cut out a selection of photographs from newspapers and magazines featuring well-known people – singers, sportsmen, politicians, TV stars, and so on. You could also include some photographs of animals. Ask the children to draw some speech bubbles on these pictures and then write in what they think the people could be saying. There will be some very amusing results that should be discussed at the end of the session.

Verse patterns

Haiku

_____

_____

_____

Tanka

_____

_____

_____

_____

_____

Cinquain

_____

_____

_____

_____

_____

Treasure hunt

Photocopiables

Prefixes and suffixes score card

Prefixes	Suffixes
Total:	Total:

Punctuation score card

Capital letters	Commas	Exclamation marks	Question marks	Full stops
Total:	Total:	Total:	Total:	Total:

Skills Grid — NATIONAL STANDARDS FOR KEY SKILLS

ACTIVITIES	Alphabetical order	Acronyms	Letter sounds	Spelling accuracy	Dictionary use	Anagrams	Vocabulary extension	Puns	Singulars and plurals	Personal pronouns	Collective nouns	Prefixes and suffixes	Syllabification	Verbs	Adverbs	Adjectives	Sentence building	Similes	Punctuation	Skim-reading	Using context cues	Understanding text types	Poetic forms	Story building	Comprehension	Reasoning, hypothesising	Co-operation	Concentration	Problem solving	Imagination, creativity	Questioning	Reading accuracy	Fluency, confidence
SECTION 1																																	
Alphabet game	✔																										✔						
The three syllable game													✔																				
Invented acronyms		✔																															
Travellers' tales	✔		✔		✔																												
Finger alphabet messages				✔																													
Anagrams, addagrams...					✔	✔																											
Singing letters			✔																														
Ghost				✔																													
Alphabetical suitcase	✔																											✔					
Secret messages	✔																												✔				
Lions and tigers			✔																							✔							
Alphabet assassination			✔	✔	✔																												
Silent *e* stories			✔																														
SECTION 2																																	
Hidden words													✔																				
Verb detective														✔																	✔		
Guess the adverb														✔	✔																		
Word walls							✔																										
Reading races							✔													✔													
Fictionary					✔		✔																							✔			
Singular and plural									✔																								
Comparative and...															✔	✔																	
Happy pronoun families										✔																							
A mash of potatoes											✔																						
List crazy							✔																										✔
Alliterative names			✔														✔																
Beginnings and endings												✔																					
Spoonerisms			✔																														
Squeezed words																														✔			
Terrific titles								✔																						✔			
SECTION 3																																	
Why, what, who...																									✔						✔		
Satisfactory sentences																	✔										✔	✔					
Tongue-twister...																	✔																
Plausible proverbs																														✔			
Improving sentences							✔																										
New similes																		✔															
Name sentences																	✔																
O'Grady says																												✔				✔	
Cloze races																					✔											✔	
SECTION 4																																	
Comprehension puzzles																									✔	✔							
Two truths and a lie																											✔						
Cut-up poetry																							✔										
Quatrains and cinquains													✔										✔										
Dramatic punctuation																			✔													✔	
Treasure hunt											✔		✔	✔																			
The writing frame game																								✔						✔			
Fabulous fiction																								✔						✔			
Crazy cartoons																								✔						✔			

Ready to go! WORD GAMES FOR LITERACY